I0818360

PERSPIRE TO GREATNESS

PERSPIRE TO GREATNESS

GOALS ARE MADE TO BE CRUSHED

JIM ROWLEY

PROUD MARINE,
CEO - CRUNCH FITNESS

Perspire to Greatness

Published by RESULTS Faster! Publishing
in Flower Mound, TX

Editing by Adept Content Solutions

Content Development by Nonie Jobe

Cover Design by Avery Hill

Printed in the United States of America

Hardcover 978-1-968127-52-7

Softcover: 978-1-968127-50-3

CONTENTS

"People do not really want freedom because freedom involves responsibility and most people are frightened of responsibility. They prefer to live under someone else's idea of truth, to obey rather than to think, to blame rather than to act. The real battle is not between good and evil, but between cowardice and courage, between those who dare to think for themselves and those who choose the comfort of the chains."

—Dostoevsky

DEDICATION AND INTRODUCTION

This book is dedicated to my mother,
Linda J. Rowley (Robinson).

She was just seventeen when she gave birth to my identical twin brother, Dave (my inspiration for joining the fitness business), and me. Married to my father, a nineteen-year-old US Marine doing everything he could to support his young family, she faced adulthood faster than most. Nine months pregnant and a senior in high school, she walked her graduation ceremony in full cap and gown. Whenever I think about determination and courage, that image of her crossing the stage always comes to mind.

I grew up surrounded by stories of service. Both of my grandfathers retired from the Navy after twenty years, and my paternal grandfather served as a Navy Corpsman attached to Marine units for nearly his entire career. My father rarely spoke in detail about his own time as a Marine, but he set the foundation for me to want to serve; when I discovered his boot camp yearbook at sixteen, something ignited in me. I poured over every page, every photo, and soon became consumed by all things military: wearing camouflage and watching *Apocalypse Now*, *The Deer Hunter*, and *The Green Berets* late into the night. I knew then that becoming a US Marine was my calling.

During my service, I had the honor of working alongside remarkable leaders and Marines who shaped my life: my Drill Instructors of Platoon 3037: SSgt. Patrick Murphy; Captain Etter of 4th Logistics Battalion (where I served on Inspector/Instructor duty); Lt. Rhodes of 2nd Battalion, 5th Marines; GySgt. "Spanky" Feest; and my friend to this day, Sgt. Felix Trevino.

While stationed in Madrid, Spain, I received a Red Cross notification that changed my life: My mother had been diagnosed with Stage IV breast cancer. As the oldest of four children and with my parents divorced, the Marine Corps returned me to the US, assigning me to the Concord Naval Weapons Station so I could care for her. I worked from 7 am to 4 pm, then spent every evening taking her to medical appointments and tending to her needs. After I put her to bed I worked at a local gym from 8 p.m. to 12 am to earn extra money. After six months of fighting, my mother, only forty years old, passed away. I was twenty-two. Losing the strongest, most loving, and most resilient person in my life was devastating. A few weeks later, I deployed to Kuwait for the Persian Gulf War.

> "The whole challenge of life is to act with honor and hope and generosity. You can't help when or what you were born, and you may not be able to help how you die; but you can and you should try to pass the days between as a good man."
>
> – Anton Myrer, *Once an Eagle*

I share this because adversity, loss, and uncertainty visit us all. And when they do, we face a choice: **to keep going or to quit.**

In 1987, I met a beautiful young woman who would later become my wife. Two years before my mother's passing, Michelle spent precious time with her while I was stationed in Nigeria and Spain. Their bond grew quickly; and through that connection, I realized I had met the second remarkable woman in my life: someone filled with joy, love, strength, grace, and unwavering determination.

In 1992, after leaving the Marine Corps and briefly pouring concrete for my brother-in-law (to whom I'm grateful for the opportunity), I applied for a "rookie sales counselor" position at 24 Hour Nautilus. I was hired by Rose Olsen, who later became a dear friend to this day; and I began at the bottom, learning to sell, learning a new way to lead, and learning to grow, personally and professionally. What followed was the foundation of more than three decades of building teams, strategies, and systems to win in the fitness industry.

I owe tremendous gratitude to those who shaped my journey, especially those who inspired me, challenged me, and even those who taught me what *not* to do.

UFC GYM (FOUNDED 2008)

As a co-founder of UFC GYM, a brand that really tested us with finding the customer appeal and haromony between UFC Fans, MMA fans, and fitness enthusiasts, I want to share my deepest gratitude to the original team of founders and leaders at UFC GYM: Lorenzo Fertitta, Frank Fertitta, Dana White, Adam Sedlack, Shawna Winters, Steve Stonehouse, and the numerous leaders and managers who started with the brand at its inception and have continued to grow the company to incredible heights. Starting something from an idea that Mark had, to meet with the UFC, who provided an opportunity for us to develop that idea into a fitness disruptor integratiing all things UFC, MMA, and Fitness was one of the highlights of my career. Additionally, the partnerships that were formed there that have turned into friendships with BJ Penn and Urijah Faber are of special note.

24 HOUR FITNESS

Thanks to Rose Olsen, Erich Jenkins, Jim Hanzalik, Tony Hernandez, Vinnie Farrell, Curtis Harman, Mark Polli, Steve Block, Brian Bouma, Derek Gallup, Mike Feeney, Neal Spruce, Mike Sheehan, Ron Thompson, Steve Clinefelter, John Romeo, Don Harbich, Sadie Lincoln, Nadine Quiroz, Gil Freeman, my Fitness Teams in the early 2000s and the countless teammates whose names aren't listed but whose impact remains deeply appreciated.

CRUNCH

My professional home and passion since 2009, where we went from bankruptcy to becoming the fastest-growing fitness franchise in the world. Words fall short in expressing the pride I feel in leading this brand. To those who were with us at the beginning and those who stand with us today, thank you. We suffered, we celebrated, and we built something extraordinary together.

Keith Worts, Ben Midgley, Brian Calegari, Amber Martinez, Craig Pepin-Donat, Donna Cyrus, Mike Blouin, Christina de Guardia, John DeMatteo, Tony Bakos, Amita Balla, Frank Pasquale, Lynn Cunningham, Marc Santa Maria, the teams at Angelo Gordon and TPG, and my current leadership team: Chequan Lewis, Dan Gallagher, Molly Long, John Tate, Alexis Bianco, Chad Waetzig, Pam Brown, John D'Anna, Mike Neff, Laura Sparks, and Christopher Flowers. And to the teams that make everything work, our field leaders, managing day in and day out to rise to the occasion, setting the bar of excellence.

A special note of thanks for the journey I have shared with Alex Wiesner (mi Hermano), Chris Dedicik, and Selena and Lusiano Afeaki. Your partnerships have only been surpassed by your friendships.

Thank you **Mark Mastrov**, the founder of 24 Hour Nautilus/ Fitness, for an early opportunity that altered my path, and for the many years that followed. Life, like partnerships, is rarely simple; but I recognize the role that beginning played in this work.

Lastly, and most importantly, to my children: **Jordan, Jake, and Taylor**. Over the years, I've found many sources of motivation, but none compared to you. Every effort to be a better father, husband, professional, leader, friend, coach, and sometimes the enforcer of reason comes from my determination never to let you down. Watching you grow into people defined by faith, family, fun, love, and trust has been the greatest joy of my life.

This book, in many ways, is for all of you.

When I look back on my journey from eight years as a Marine to more than three decades in the fitness industry, I see one lesson repeated over and over again: Leadership decides everything.

We've built Crunch into a thriving network of more than 500 gyms across the globe. That growth didn't happen because of luck. It didn't happen because corporate parachuted in with answers. It happened because franchise owners, general managers, and teams stepped up, took responsibility, and refused to quit. Like I often say, **"No one is coming. It's up to you to form the winning team. It's up to you to drive that team to excellence."**

This book is for all of you who make Crunch what it is today:

- Franchisees who bet on this brand and put your name on the line in your communities
- Leaders of teams (fifty to a hundred strong in every club) who show up daily to serve members and chase goals
- Prospective owners who are considering joining our family and need to know what it really takes
- Friends, colleagues, strategic partners, and history keepers who have been part of this journey from bankruptcy days to where we stand now

But this book isn't just for the Crunch family. It's also for every franchise owner, operator, and leader out there, no matter the industry, who wants to build something special. If you're leading a team, growing a brand, or trying to create a culture that lasts, what's inside these pages applies to you. The principles that drive our success at Crunch (clarity of vision, meticulous execution, servant leadership, and a relentless focus on people) translate across every business.

It's for the entrepreneur who's betting on themselves for the first time. For the seasoned operator who's looking to reignite purpose and passion in their organization. For the leaders who believe "culture eats strategy for breakfast," and who want to know how to build one that wins. And it's for anyone who's hungry to learn what it really takes to scale a business without losing the heart, determination, and community that made it great in the first place.

I want this book to be a companion. Something you can flip open for inspiration, and something you can use as a teaching tool with your own teams. Inside you'll find principles, frameworks, and stories that reflect how we've built Crunch from 36 struggling clubs into a thriving system that exports talent, creates careers, and inspires members every single day.

As you read, you're going to notice certain words, phrases, and ideas show up more than once. That's not an accident. When something is critical to your development as a leader, I want it to stick, so I come back to it. It may feel repetitive at times, and that's intentional. Repetition is the mother of learning. When you see a theme or a phrase return again and again, let it remind you that this is exactly how real learning sticks.

The Marine in me still believes in grit, discipline, and toughness. We don't make excuses. We don't wait around, so you will see that part of me throughout; get ready.

For example, **"Figure it the F out. Don't let a roadblock stop you."** That mindset carried me from the barracks to the boardroom, and it's the same mindset that will carry Crunch into its next decade of growth.

Here's what you can expect in the pages ahead:

- We'll start by calling out the leadership vacuum. It's why so many managers wait for rescue and why that's deadly for performance.
- We'll talk **about culture and persistence** and why surrounding yourself with people who bring energy, humility, and commitment is non-negotiable.
- We'll dig into leadership DNA: why résumés don't matter nearly as much as character, loyalty, and the will to finish.
- You'll see how everyday people can achieve above-average results with the right systems, training, and standards.
- You'll hear how character, authenticity, and never quitting have been the backbone of Crunch's success. And you'll see key ideas and strategies repeated to ensure that they are cemented in your learning.

Think of this as a field manual rather than just a book full of abstract theories. They're battle-tested principles, frameworks, and lessons. Some are from the Marines, some from late nights on the road building gyms, and some from the hard years when we bought Crunch out of bankruptcy and had to close clubs just to survive.

This is a collection of insights I've absorbed, They're not all original to me, but they've become part of my playbook. They're the performance metrics I've used to lead teams, drive sales organizations, hit goals, and navigate the inevitable challenges that come when you're building something that matters. Think of this as a tool for inspiration but for execution as well. If you're willing to dig in, this can help you do some of the very things I've spent the last thirty-three years learning. While this book is primarily focused on the fitness industry and the Marine Corps, the practices, skills, and standards that this book will impart on you cross indutries and fields.

Scared money don't make money. That principle has guided every risk we've taken, from franchising our first new clubs to scaling across continents.

"Scared money don't make money."

I'm proud of what we've built, but I'm even more excited about where we're going. With every new franchisee who signs on, every team member who puts on a Crunch uniform, and every member who chooses us over the competition, we are writing the next chapter together.

So read this book not just as a history, but as a challenge. A challenge to take ownership. A challenge to build highly capable teams that win again and again. A challenge to never quit, even when the odds are stacked.

We've come this far thanks to the sheer fortitude and effort of many people. I hope the pages ahead will give you tools you can use, stories that inspire, and a vision that makes you proud to be part of Crunch or whatever company you're leading.

What I hope every reader takes away from this book, whether you're a club owner, a general manager, a CEO, an entrepreneur, or just someone curious about what makes great organizations work, is that it captures more than three decades of strategy, performance, and decision-making. My goal is to save you some of the trial and error that come with leadership by sharing what has been tested, what has worked, and what has endured. Think of it as best practices built in the real world, not a classroom.

Let me also be clear about something: Not everything I have tried or written about in this book has always worked. It has taken decades for these ideas to come together in a way that makes sense. Along the way I've hired the wrong people, failed to train and develop them the way they deserved, and missed chances to recognize them. We have launched brands that didn't make it, and I've lost money. I often say, "Scared money don't make money," and I believe that; but I have also been on the other side when a bet didn't pay off. This has not been a thirty-three-year run of straight ten out of ten wins.

One example: I was part of a joint venture that opened clubs around the world. We grew to ten or twelve locations and financed part of it with debt to a group in Europe. When that group defaulted on their debt, the company collapsed. It was painful, expensive, and humbling. The point is this: What you are holding in your hands is the product of both successes and failures, not some perfect theory.

These lessons are tried and true but they only work when they're led by effective people. That's where personal accountability comes in. Reading about strategy or culture isn't enough; you have to apply it, measure it, and stay committed to it. Leadership isn't a title. It's a responsibility.

Everything in these pages reflects what's worked for me and the teams I've led. It may not look exactly the same in your world; every company has its own culture, every leader their own style, but the principles are universal. They're transformational when you commit to them.

If I'd had something like this thirty years ago, a roadmap for building culture, shaping strategy, leading teams, and hiring the right people, it would've saved me a lot of learning the hard way. The idea that "it's the DNA, not the résumé" didn't come overnight; it came from years of hiring, coaching, and discovering what truly drives performance.

So, I offer this book as a way to give you a head start. It's the relative intelligence of someone who's been there—who's succeeded, stumbled, learned, and kept moving forward. I hope what's inside helps you take one more confident step ahead in your own journey of leadership and excellence.

After more than three decades in the fitness business, I've recognized that people don't understand what it takes. They only see the success. They don't see the million miles on the commercial airlines, the midnight flights, the grind. But that's what it takes to build something that lasts.

Now let's get to work.

Part I

THE STATE OF LEADERSHIP TODAY

Leadership starts with personal responsibility and mental toughness. No one is coming to help you, so you must own the outcome and build a team culture resilient enough to win. It takes Grit and Determination.

Chapter 1

WHERE HAVE ALL THE LEADERS GONE?

"No one is coming. It's really up to you to form the winning team. It's up to you to drive that team to excellence."

—Jim Rowley

Walk into almost any organization today and you'll find managers waiting for someone else to fix the problem. They blame headquarters. They blame the market. They wait for someone to show up and rescue the team. That's not leadership. That's dependency.

In my years both in the fitness business and in the Marines, I've seen the same pattern over and over: Teams flounder when leaders assume salvation is coming from outside. The truth? **No one is coming. You are it.**

The success of your team, your department, your gym, your business rests on your shoulders.

When I first stepped into management roles at 24 Hour Fitness, the instinct was to lean on "corporate" whenever something went wrong. If you want to consistently win and if you want your team to deliver results month after month, you can't outsource leadership. You must own it. At the end of the day, success or failure depends on the leader in the club.

The message landed because people wanted to believe that if they just followed the process, results would come automatically. But the reality is different. You can have the best marketing, the best sales scripts, the best equipment; but if you don't have a leader taking ownership, you'll never hit goal consistently. If you want a winning team, it starts with you.

Leaders today face a double challenge. On one hand, we live in a culture that's gotten soft, quick to complain, quick to make excuses. On the other hand, the demands of business have never been more relentless. Competition is global, technology changes weekly, and customers have endless choices. Weak leadership collapses under that pressure. Strong leadership thrives on it.

No one is coming. You are it.

THE WAITING TRAP

Too many organizations are virtually stuck because their leadership is waiting to be rescued. You hear it in their meetings. They talk in vague motivation, not real plans.

The Marine Corps taught me that leadership isn't about position; it's about responsibility. When you're leading a unit in the field, there is no passing the buck. You don't wait for a memo from Washington to decide how to react under fire. You take responsibility. You act. You lead.

That same mindset applies in business. You don't wait for corporate to solve your staffing issues. You don't wait for the economy to turn around. You don't wait for permission to build a winning culture. Leadership is stepping up, taking responsibility, and owning the outcome, even when it would be easier to point fingers.

One of the quickest ways to recognize a team that's waiting to be rescued is to sit quietly in their weekly meeting and just observe. You can learn more about a team's leadership health in one meeting than in a month of reports. Almost immediately, you can see who's leading and who's drifting. I look for the level of preparation, the quality of discussion, and the intent behind the conversation. Are they walking in with data? Have they been analyzing their business? Do they have a strategy and just as important, a course correction when things aren't working? Have they identified their problems, understood the root causes, and written a plan to fix them? Are they training against that plan, tracking progress, and holding each other accountable with measurable results?

Strong teams meet with purpose. Weak teams meet out of habit. Too often, when a team is sitting around waiting for someone else to come fix things, there's no substance in the conversation: no direction, no data, no plan. Just motivational talk. "We need to work harder." Working harder isn't a strategy.

I remember back in the nineties, that was the default answer in our clubs. I'd ask, "How are you going to hit goal this month?" and they'd tell me, "We're going to rock." That kind of false motivation used to drive me crazy. Energy's great; but without a plan, it's just noise. So I started writing checklists. I taught teams how to write a real strategy: time-bound, data-driven, and measurable. Simple, smart planning. And it changed everything. We went from struggling to hit goals to growing our personal training business from $90 million to $300 million.

S	Specific	Make your goal specific and narrow for more effective planning.
M	Measurable	Make sure your goal and progress are measurable.
A	Achievable	Make sure you can reasonably accomplish your goal within a certain time frame.
R	Relevant	Your goal should align with your values and long-term objectives
T	Time-based	Set a realistic but ambitious end date to clarify task prioritization and increase motivation

That shift didn't come from working harder; it came from thinking smarter. From leading with data instead of emotion. Because if you're not talking about data points (which in our business is leads, guests, closing ratios, average per sale, re-sign behaviors) you're flying blind. We have the advantage of having more data than most companies. The numbers tell a story every single day, but you have to go into discovery mode. You have to dig for the patterns, identify the gaps, and build a plan to fix them.

Leads
Appointments
Shows
Enrollment
Referrals

Use the LASER framework to help you lead.

Teams that wait to be rescued believe change will just happen if they show up. But leadership doesn't work that way. Things don't change for the sake of change. They change when leaders decide to own the problem, study the data, and take action with intention.

Ask yourself right now: Are you leading like someone who's waiting to be rescued, or are you leading like someone who knows it's up to them?

Great leaders aren't defined by their job titles, their perks, or their résumés. They're defined by their willingness to accept responsibility when others shy away. They're the ones who can say to their teams with conviction: "Follow me. I've got this. We'll figure it out."

I believe great leaders share seven common traits:

- They have vision
- They are results-oriented

- They are innovative
- They are courageous
- They lead with integrity
- They lead by example
- They practice emotional intelligence

Vision: A vision isn't a statement; it's a set of ideas that describe a future state. A true vision should be dynamic, driving continuous learning and innovation while serving as a guiding light for you and your team. But vision alone isn't enough; it must be anchored by purpose: a clear, well-thought-out mission that keeps everyone aligned when the road gets tough. A strong mission simplifies the hard calls because it defines what matters most. It speaks of goal setting, which keeps the vision focused; training, which builds the capability to deliver it; and accountability, which, though it's often the hardest part, ensures it actually happens.

Ask yourself:

- *Where do we want to be?*
- *How do I/we want to be viewed?*

Results-oriented: Being results-oriented means more than just wanting success; it means directing your energy and focus toward what truly matters. Your vision must move you in a clear direction, one that's defined by meaningful results. Know which outcomes are most important and align your time, people, and resources to achieve them. Set clear goals, plan intentionally, and take deliberate action every day to move closer to those goals. Then measure your progress. Because if you can't measure it, you can't manage it; and if you can't manage it, you can't sustain it. Leaders who win are those who make results visible, measurable, and repeatable.

Ask yourself:

- *What are my key responsibilities?*
- *Have I trained my team to achieve the mission?* (As a leader, you cannot ask anyone to do anything unless you have prepared them for it.)
- *What actions must I take to achieve the desired results?*
- *Do I have a back-up plan? Can I improvise?*

Innovative: Being innovative means never settling for "good enough." It's about constantly striving to improve, because if you keep doing the same thing, you'll keep getting the same result. That's fine only if you're already achieving at the highest level. True leaders challenge themselves first, knowing their teams will follow their example. Innovation starts with self-awareness, particularly the courage to admit when a plan isn't working and the ability to adapt quickly. Learn from the past, plan for the future, and manage in the present. Great leaders stay curious; they expose themselves to new ideas, seek fresh perspectives from their teams, and identify the winners worth pursuing. Change is inevitable, and in most cases, you'll be the one driving it. If you're not, someone else will drive it for you.

Ask yourself:

- *What have I learned in the last month?*
- *What have I done with what I have learned?*

- *Where can I improve?*
- *Where will I find the answer on how to improve?*

Courageous: Being courageous is the mark of a true leader. Courage isn't the absence of fear; it's the decision to move forward in spite of it. There are four types of courage every leader must develop:

1. The courage to make hard decisions in those moments that test your judgment, decisiveness, integrity, and knowledge.
2. The courage to be patient, understanding that results and clarity don't always come on your timeline.
3. The courage to face difficult situations head-on, whether it's a critical conversation or crucial confrontation. The key is preparation; plan those conversations instead of improvising in the heat of emotion.
4. The courage to admit when you're wrong and take action to make it right.

Leaders experience the same fears as everyone else; the difference is, they take the next step anyway.

Ask yourself:

- *What decision am I avoiding right now?*
- *Where do I need to act despite uncertainty or fear?*
- *What difficult conversation have I been putting off?*
- *Am I fully prepared to handle the tough situations I face?*
- *When was the last time I admitted I was wrong—and what did I do about it?*

> "Don't replace your backbone with a wishbone."
> *–Elizabeth Gilbert*

Integrity: Being a leader with integrity means your word is your bond; it's something people can take to the bank. A handshake should still mean something. Integrity shows up, not in what you say but in whether you follow through, especially when it's difficult. Say what you're going to do and do it; and, just as importantly, do it *when* you said you would. This is where courage meets character. Following up on both discipline and rewards is critical, because nothing kills respect faster than duplicity or inconsistency. Integrity also means surrounding yourself with truth-tellers, not "yes" men or "yes" women.

In my early years as a district manager, I saw firsthand how quickly trust disappears when a leader treats their word casually. We had just won Region of the Year three years in a row. Each time, the regional vice president of sales received a Rolex as part of his recognition. Going into the fourth year, he told me and another district manager, "If we win again, I am going to give each of you a Rolex. I already have mine."

We took that seriously. We pushed hard, rallied our teams, and we won that fourth year. No watches. No explanation. The promise just vanished. To this day, the other district manager and I still laugh about it; but the truth is, it left a mark. At the beginning of this book, I said there are people I learned what to do from and people I learned what not to do from. He is in that second group.

What he taught me, by negative example, is that when a leader offers recognition or a reward and then does not deliver, it breaks more than a promise. It damages trust. It cheapens future recognition. It tells people that what you say does not really matter. Later in this book, I talk about the importance of recognizing people for doing what you ask of them. This is the other side of that coin. When you promise recognition, whether it is a watch, a bonus, a promotion, or a simple public thank you, you have to honor it. The way you recognize and reward people is not separate from integrity. It is one of the clearest tests of it.

With *each decision*, ask yourself:

- *Would I be proud to have this action publicly known for the rest of my career?*

Lead by example: Leading by example is the foundation of all real leadership. Your team will mirror what they see in you: your attitude, your behaviors, your values, and your opinions. There are three types of teams: incapable, capable, and highly capable. Which one you have depends largely on what they see from you day to day. As a leader, you live in a fishbowl. People notice everything: the time you arrive, the time you leave, when you're in a good mood, when you're not, who your favorites are, and what truly matters to you. Every action communicates something. Use the Coaching Loop to build consistency and clarity: Tell them, show them, ask them to repeat it back, have them coach you, then repeat and hold them accountable. Leadership doesn't take days off. Consistency builds credibility, and credibility builds trust.

Ask yourself:

- *If everyone on my team acted just like me, would we perform better?*
- *Do I consistently set the right example?*
- *Are there things I can change?*

Emotional Intelligence: Practicing emotional intelligence is one of the most powerful traits of an effective leader. It's the ability to be aware of your own emotions, to control and express them appropriately, and to manage relationships with empathy and good judgment. There are five key components to emotional intelligence. You must be:

1. **Self-aware** – Understand your emotions and how they affect your thoughts and behavior.

2. **Self-regulating** – Control impulses, think before acting, and stay consistent under stress.

3. **Self-motivating** – Maintain focus, energy, and optimism, even when the road gets tough.

4. **Empathetic** – Listen well and understand others' perspectives before responding.

5. **Socially skilled** – Communicate with humility, charm, and energy that draws people in.

Additionally, here's an acronym I developed that I believe defines the difference between "good" and "great" leaders:

Committed: Dedication and loyalty to your cause, an activity, or a job

Responsible: Assuming an obligation to do something or having control over or caring for someone as part of your job or role

Unified: To make or become united, uniform, or whole

> **And U**nafraid: Scared money don't make money.

Nimble (like a Ninja): Employing quick and light movement or action, moving around, developing quick thinking, and staying alert

Courageous: The ability to do something that frightens you or having strength in the face of pain

Humble: Having or showing a modest or low estimate of your own self-importance

> **And H**ardworking: Nothing worth gaining is easy.

The CRUNCH acronym was heavily influenced by my time in the Marines. In addition to the seven common traits of good leaders, please consider some or all of the following as they resonate with you.

MARINE CORPS CORE VALUES

Honor—exemplifying ethical and moral behavior
Courage—the ability to proceed with calmness and firmness in the face of danger or criticism
Commitment—a dedication to carrying out tasks and serving the values of the Corps and the country

LEADERSHIP PRINCIPLES

Be technically and tactically proficient.
Know yourself and seek self-improvement.
Know your Marines and look out for their welfare.
Ensure knowledge and competence are shared within the unit.
Set the example.
Make sound and timely decisions.
Employ your unit and Marines in a timely and conservative manner.
Develop a sense of responsibility in your Marines for their actions.

LEADERSHIP TRAITS

Bearing
Courage
Decisiveness
Dependability
Endurance
Enthusiasm
Initiative
Integrity
Judgment
Justice
Knowledge
Loyalty
Tact
Unselfishness

LEADERSHIP IDENTITY SHIFT: FROM MILITARY TO BUSINESS

I fought early in my career to lead like a Marine: direct, aggressive, absolute. But I had to learn something critical: **You can't lead civilians like you lead Marines. You can't just bark orders and expect buy-in. I had to reframe my leadership style from being a disciplinarian to becoming a coach.**

You're never going to leave the Marine Corps and become a civilian. *You become a veteran.* Those values (discipline, honor, taking care of your people) don't leave. But the methods must shift. Leadership in business requires translation: Less aggression, more adaptability. Less command, more coaching. You have to take the best of your old identity—the values, the principles—and find a way to make them work in a different environment, one where people haven't been through the same kind of training or shared the same experiences.

> "Be a coach, not a cop."
>
> *–Jim Rowley*

I eventually realized I wasn't leading Marines anymore. These were civilians, talented people who hadn't gone through that same crucible of leadership training. So when I led with that same intensity, it didn't land. It came off as hard, even harsh. That understanding was the turning point for me; I realized that I'd never lose that Marine identity, but that I had to translate it.

It wasn't about softening my standards; it was about smoothing the sharp edges so the message could connect.

People sometimes ask me, "Do you try to instill that same kind of identity in your team?" The answer is yes; but it's not about turning them into Marines. It's about instilling the same characteristics that make great Marines *and* great leaders.

The Marine Corps teaches aggression, and that was probably the first thing I had to unlearn. In the military, aggression isn't about anger; it's about decisive action. You're trained to move toward the problem, not away from it. When you're under fire, the instinct for most people is to seek cover, to hide, to wait. But Marines are trained through repetition to do the opposite: to identify, advance, and resolve. That mindset becomes instinct.

In the civilian world, that level of aggression doesn't translate. You can't lead a sales team or build a business by charging forward the same way you would in combat. But the *principle* behind it still holds true. In the face of adversity, when things go wrong or when plans fall apart, you move forward. You don't freeze. You don't dwell. You adapt and take the next step.

That's where most people stumble. When they hit resistance, they stop to analyze, to question, to overthink. They let doubt creep in. They get stuck in "What now?" instead of moving toward "What's next?" The Marine Corps trained me to act, not recklessly, but with conviction and momentum. That's what I've tried to carry into leadership in business.

You lose your best salesperson? Move forward. The market shifts overnight? Move forward. The numbers aren't where you want them to be? Move forward. The mission doesn't stop because circumstances change. That's the mindset I brought with me, and it's the one I try to instill in every leader I coach.

That shift starts with building trust before demanding performance. It's why we use the **Coaching Loop**:

1. You *set the expectation.* You clearly define what "great" looks like.
2. You *teach to the expectation.* You walk them through it, explain the "why," and show what it looks like in action.
3. You *have them teach it back.* If they can't articulate it, they don't own it.
4. You *hold them accountable,* because what gets measured, gets done.

Simple. Repeatable. Effective.

Let me give you an example from my personal experience. I remember working with a team member named Amber Martinez. Back when she was running YogaWorks for me, she was stepping into her first big leadership role. Amber was talented, passionate, and hardworking; but like a lot of new leaders, she didn't yet have a full grasp of the Profit & Loss Statement. It was a gap that showed up quickly, and I could see that if she didn't learn to own those numbers, it would limit how far she could go.

So we sat down together and went line by line through that P&L. We broke down what each number meant, how it connected to strategy, and why it mattered to performance. Then, to her credit, she didn't stop there. Over the next month, she studied it. She asked questions. She connected the dots between the numbers and her daily decisions. She started to see how every move—every staffing decision, every expense, every operational tweak—showed up on that statement.

In time, she became an expert. Not just at reading a P&L, but at using it to run her business. And when she transitioned to Crunch, that expertise carried over. She no longer needed someone telling her where the problems were. She saw them herself. She built strategies around them. She became proactive instead of reactive.

I believe Amber will tell you today that was one of the biggest breakthrough moments of her career. Learning to truly understand the bottom line gave her confidence, credibility, and control. And that's what leadership is about. Great leaders don't wait to be told where the gaps are. They find them, fix them, and build better systems because of it.

That's leadership: not waiting to be taught but becoming a student of what matters.

GENERATION GAP OR LEADERSHIP GAP?

I've spent a lot of time thinking about the generational gap in leadership. About ten or fifteen years ago, I put together a two-hour presentation on managing across generations: Boomers, Gen X, Millennials, and now Gen Z and Alphas. I used movie clips, music, and technology from each era. The contrast was eye-opening. What Boomers and Gen X grew up seeing and hearing on screen—how they communicated, how they viewed authority—was worlds apart from what Millennials and Gen Z have experienced. The tone, the speed, the expectations, even the humor all shifted dramatically.

Older generations were raised to believe success was a straight climb: You get a good job, stay loyal, work hard, and retire with a pension. That was the playbook. **But for the younger generations, it's a jungle gym, not a ladder.** They move laterally, change jobs every year or two, want open communication, and expect direct access to leadership. And they ask *why*: Why are we doing this, why does it matter, why should I give my Saturday for it? That's not defiance; it's curiosity. It's a different lens on purpose.

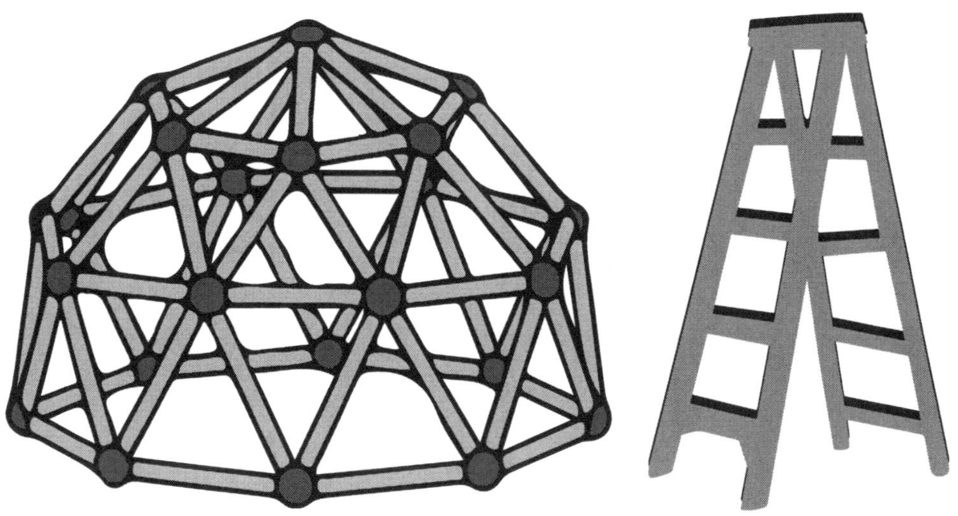

But the truth is, no matter what generation you're from, everyone still wants the same core things. They want to be recognized. They want opportunity. And they want to be led. That's the common ground that never changes. Whether you're 58 or 28, that's the bridge. The need for strong leadership transcends the generation gap. The idea that young people don't want to be led is just wrong. They want leaders who are consistent, fair, and worth following.

And that's where leadership today has to step up. Because leadership, at its core, is about discipline. It's about doing the things you don't always want to do, every single day. That's true in every part of life: your work, your fitness, your relationships. Discipline is doing what's right when nobody's watching. It's saying no to the easy path. It's respecting yourself and others enough to stay focused.

The problem today isn't that people don't want success; it's that too many want the reward without the work. Everyone wants to eat; not everyone wants to hunt. But unless you were born with a silver spoon or a trust fund, life requires the hunt. You have to get up, show up, and lead yourself before you can lead others.

That's what separates those who wait to be led from those who become the next generation of leaders. The ones who will fill the gap are the ones willing to put in the effort every day, not just when it's convenient.

"There's no substitute for hard work."

—Jim Rowley

That's really the question this chapter is getting at. It's not that the next generation doesn't have potential; they absolutely do. It's that too few people are showing them what real leadership looks like. Somewhere along the way, the standards slipped. We stopped teaching discipline, accountability, and ownership, and started settling for participation and positivity. Leadership isn't about managing feelings; it's about setting direction, creating clarity, and building people who can carry the torch forward. If we want to close the leadership gap, we have to stop waiting for the old playbook to come back and start writing a new one: one that's rooted in timeless principles, but adapted to today's world. That's where the next great wave of leaders will come from.

TOOL: THE LEADERSHIP SELF-CHECK

Write down one leadership challenge you currently face. Then ask:

- ***Where am I waiting instead of leading?***
- ***What part of this situation do I own?***
- ***What action can I take within the next 24 hours?***

Stop waiting. Start leading.

TOOL: THE OWNERSHIP LADDER

Step 1: Excuses—*It's not my fault.*

Step 2: Blame—*If only corporate/my boss/the market did X.*

Step 3: Acknowledgment—*I had a role in this outcome.*

Step 4: Responsibility—*It's on me to fix this.*

Step 5: Ownership—*The result is mine to deliver. Period.*

Leaders who climb this ladder stop asking, *Who will help me?* and start saying, *What can I do right now?*

Credited to Bruce Gordon.

EXERCISE: OWNERSHIP AUDIT

List the top three problems in your business right now. Next to each:

- Circle "Waiting" if you expect someone else to solve it.
- Circle "Owning" if you're actively leading the fix.

Shift one "Waiting" to "Owning" this week and build a real plan to close the gap.

> "Working harder isn't a strategy.
> Leading with intention is."
> *–Jim Rowley*

The following points make up the most important takeaways for this chapter. They will be located at the end of each chapter of the book for your reference.

CHAPTER 1 VERY IMPORTANT POINTS

- Leadership starts the moment you accept that no one is coming to save you.
- Excuses kill execution; ownership accelerates results.
- Data must drive direction or you're flying blind.
- Weak teams wait. Strong teams prepare, analyze, and act.
- Leadership is responsibility, not rescue.

CRUNCH

Chapter 2

REBUILDING A CULTURE OF HIGH STANDARDS

"This is the great filter. Everybody says they want greatness. Great love. Great health. Great life. Great contribution. But very few allow themselves to undergo what is required to be great. Greatness doesn't care about skill. Greatness doesn't care about experience. Greatness doesn't care about talent. Greatness only asks us to *give it our all*. And the only person that knows whether you've left it all on the table or played it safe *is you*. So lean in. On the other side of the burn, on the other side of the resistance, on the other side of the challenges, is your power."

—Branden Collinsworth

Let's be honest: Discipline is becoming rare. More and more people in business fold under pressure, complain about circumstances, or search for reasons something didn't go their way. And that mindset spreads fast through teams, through companies, even through entire industries.

That's why the first thing I look for in any team or franchise isn't talent. It's whether the culture is built on **standards strong enough to win**. And by standards, I don't mean being loud, harsh, or authoritarian. I mean **resilience, humility, consistency, and follow-through**, the ingredients that keep a team moving forward even when the plan falls apart.

The ideal operating state is simple: **No drama. No jealousy. No excuses. High standards. High effort. High respect.** People committed to bringing out the best in each other.

But how many leaders actually create that environment? Too many allow complaints, gossip, and blame to take root. And once they do, accountability evaporates and the whole team softens.

The Marines taught me a different approach. In the Corps, you don't survive by looking for easier conditions. You survive by becoming more consistent, more resourceful, and more locked into the mission every single day. Complaining about weather, equipment, or assignments was just wasted breath. I'm not saying that Marines don't complain. They do, **but they move forward anyway**. And that's what you do. You figure it out. You execute. And you take care of your people. That mindset isn't just for battle; it applies directly to business.

I've seen clubs thrive in the toughest markets, not because they had the best real estate or flashiest equipment, but because they built a **culture of high standards**. They recruited people

Everyone envies what you have, but no one envies what it took to get there. Before you succeed, people ask, "Why are you working so hard?" After you succeed, they say, "Must be nice."

–Unknown

who weren't afraid of work, who didn't expect life to be fair, and who didn't unravel at the first obstacle.

If you tolerate low standards, you get mediocre results. If you demand high standards, you get performance. And performance compounds. High-standard people attract other high-standard people; and before long, you're building something that endures.

So look at your own team and ask yourself: ***Are you leading a culture of excuses or a culture of excellence?***

Here's the decision you have to make: Most people would rather lie under the blanket of freedom than provide the blanket of freedom. You've defined what you want, but have you defined what you're willing to give to get it? Most folks want to be cared for, not be the caregiver. They want the trophy, the title, the paycheck; but when it comes to carrying responsibility, to lifting others, that part gets left behind. If you're going to truly lead, you have to opt into being the one who provides the blanket. You have to be willing to carry the weight. Because the freedom that comes with leadership is never without responsibility.

Getting your shit together requires a level of honesty you can't even imagine. There's nothing easy about realizing your'e the one that's been holding you back the whole time.

—Unknown

BUILDING A CULTURE OF EXCELLENCE

Peter Drucker famously said, "Culture eats strategy for breakfast." He was right. You can have the most brilliant business model in the world; but if the culture is broken, the wheels eventually fall off.

People sometimes say, "Our company feels like one big happy family." Usually, that means it's the most dysfunctional family in town. We're not building a family here. We're building a **team**.

And not just any team: a **high-performance** team. Offense, defense, special teams. Grinders, thinkers, builders, coaches, mentors. People aligned around mission, vision, and standards.

A winning culture is made of people who show up hungry; focused; kind; inclusive; authentic; and, most importantly, **committed**.

We're not here to carry dead weight. We're not here for drama or excuses. We're here to build something exceptional.

Yes, our brand is welcoming, offbeat, real. Yes, our values are kindness, inclusion, authenticity. But make no mistake: **We are building a culture of winners.**

I came from humble beginnings. I've made more money and achieved more than I ever dreamed as a kid. I chased material things for a while: sports cars, big houses, all of it. But here's what I finally realized: **None of that matters**. What matters is people. People are the fuel. And when I meet winners in the field, leaders who are building, producing, and raising the bar, I want more of that. Because who *doesn't* want to be part of a culture of excellence?

Now here's the real question: **Are you that kind of leader?** Are you building that kind of team? Are you setting the tone? Are you recruiting, training, and developing top talent? Are you eliminating negativity, blocking drama, and setting non-negotiable standards? Are you evaluating your people honestly? Are you showing up early, staying late, mastering all sides of your business?

Have you actually done everything required to build the culture you say you want?

Only you can answer that.

FOUR FILTERS FOR HIGH-STANDARD HIRING

When it comes to hiring, most of the problems organizations face can be eliminated right at the door if you know what to look for.

FILTER 1: WHAT TIME DID THEY SHOW UP?

You can learn a lot from that alone. If someone's late to the interview, they're already telling you how they'll treat the job.

FILTER 2: HOW DO THEY PRESENT THEMSELVES?

We're a gym brand. Nobody needs a suit, but professionalism matters. You must be clean, groomed, prepared, attentive to detail. How someone shows up reflects how seriously they take opportunity.

FILTER 3: HOW DID THEY PREPARE FOR TODAY?

That single question tells me everything I need to know about initiative. Did they research Crunch? Visit a club? Go through the sales process somewhere to understand what we do? Did they look up the person interviewing them? You can tell very quickly who's serious and who's just showing up. Preparation reveals mindset.

FILTER 4: WHAT SHAPED THEM GROWING UP?

I ask about school, sports, clubs, mentors. Were they part of a team? An individual competitor? Who coached them? What did they dream of becoming?

These aren't small-talk questions. They reveal whether someone has learned to commit, compete, and collaborate. Nearly every role we have is goal-driven. If someone has never been in an environment where performance matters, they'll struggle.

That's why hiring the right DNA matters. **Skills can be trained. Standards and accountability must already be in the wiring.**

Hire that, and you don't just fill positions. You build a culture that doesn't need rescuing.

TRAINING FOR DISCIPLINE AND ACCOUNTABILITY

Developing people who hold high standards doesn't start with yelling or raising expectations to impossible levels. It starts with who you hire, and how you lead.

This isn't about physical grit or being confrontational. It's about **courage, clarity, and consistent accountability**. It's about being the kind of leader who doesn't fold under pressure and who's willing to have direct, respectful conversations about performance and expectations.

And the first step is modeling it.

The best way to coach toughness is to be highly proficient at what you're asking others to do. If you expect someone to sell, you better be a skilled salesperson. If you expect high operational standards, you better know those standards cold. People follow competence and consistency long before they follow titles.

Real leadership means being steady when things are uncomfortable. It means saying, "Here's the expectation. Here's where we fell short. Here's how we fix it." Direct, respectful, and focused on outcomes.

The challenge is that society has drifted away from accountability in many areas—law, norms, even basic standards of behavior. That same mindset creeps into the workplace. When people start doing whatever they want, whenever they want, it leads to chaos. In any business, you have to establish what's required to be part of the team; that includes showing up on time, in uniform, ready to serve, with the right attitude. Then hold people to it. Otherwise, you're not leading; you're presiding over disorder.

And here's where a quote by Kiko Suarez rings true: **"It's not what you preach; it's what you tolerate."**

> You can't expect excellence if you're allowing exceptions.
> You can't expect accountability if you're not holding yourself to it.
> You can't preach standards you don't personally live.

Every promotion exposes new gaps. We all get promoted to our highest level of incompetence the moment we reach a role that demands skills we haven't developed yet. The leaders who succeed are the ones who learn quickly, stay humble, and stay visible.

And here's where it gets personal. You can't expect your team to be accountable if you're not holding yourself to that same level. You can't cheat on your standards and expect excellence from others. Leadership starts with the mirror. You have to be the example. You have to make the hard calls, have the tough conversations, and be willing to give up personal comfort for team success. That's the cost of leadership; it takes time, sacrifice, and constant self-awareness. Georgia Bulldogs head coach Kirby Smart identifies three specific "costs" of leadership that he keeps plastered on his desk as a reminder. He argues that while many discuss the benefits of leading, true leadership requires a willingness to accept these inherent trade-offs:

1. Making hard decisions that negatively affect people you care about. Leaders must prioritize the collective good of the organization over individual feelings, even when those individuals are close to them.
2. Being disliked despite your best attempts to do the best for the most. Smart emphasizes that leadership is not a popularity contest; even when you act with the best intentions for the majority, you will still face critics.
3. Being misunderstood without always having the opportunity to defend yourself. Leaders often operate with context or nuance that the public or team doesn't see, and they must stay grounded in their purpose even when the narrative feels unfair.

Smart's broader philosophy for managing these costs is captured in his "Confront and Demand" approach: Elite teams do not ignore mistakes, but rather confront them immediately and demand a higher standard.

Every new role introduces new challenges that expose what you don't yet know. Leadership is a goldfish bowl. Everyone sees your energy, your consistency, your effort, your courage.

Most people want to blend into the background. Leaders don't get that option.

CHOOSE YOUR HARD

Let me say something plainly: **Life is hard. Business is hard. Leadership is hard.** This is not a complaint, just reality.

Today, too many people try to engineer their lives around comfort. They want slow mornings, no pressure, plenty of time off, and they also want big titles, big checks, and big opportunities.

That math doesn't work. Greatness and comfort do not coexist.

I've seen this play out for thirty-three years. Everyone says they want success. But when pressure increases, when sacrifices are required, when weekends disappear, that's when the truth shows up.

So I tell my teams: **Choose your hard.**

> Being broke is hard.
> Hitting quota every month is also hard.
> Missing a night out is hard.
> Missing a promotion is harder.
> Maintaining standards is hard.
> Cleaning up after low standards is harder.

You choose.

Want an example? Look at a rookie on the PGA Tour—thirty-five weeks a year on the road, chasing a paycheck, paying their own way, grinding through pressure with no guarantees. That's hard.

Or the NBA—eighty-two games, constant travel, nonstop accountability. Hard.

Astronauts? They leave the planet. They're not missing their kid's soccer game. They're missing gravity. Hard.

They all made a choice: whether the challenge was worth the reward.

If you want to become a partner, run a club, get on stage, or build real wealth, you're going to have to give things up. Period.

One of the hardest choices I've ever made was the decision to go international. When many of our brands expanded into Chile, Russia, Mexico, Australia, Germany—all at the same time—it tested everything I had as a leader. It wasn't just one new market or one big trip. It was constant motion. I'd be in Australia one month, Mexico the next, Chile after that, then off to Germany and Italy. It was nonstop.

Traveling internationally sounds exciting, but it comes with real tradeoffs. You're dealing with different time zones, different cultures, and different expectations, all while trying to lead a business back home and be present for your family. Every one of those countries wanted attention, and they deserved it. So I had to be on all the time—setting strategy, leading teams, inspiring people, and doing it in multiple time zones, multiple languages, and multiple stages of development. I was fortunate to have great partners, leaders, and teams in each location.

That period stretched me more than anything else I've done in my career. It forced me to become more disciplined, more structured, and more intentional about my time and energy. It was exhausting at times, but it also reminded me what real leadership requires: showing up, staying consistent, and choosing hard when the easy option would be to pull back. That's what leadership is. You can't ask your team to give their all if you're not willing to do the same, even when it costs you.

Every day, you're choosing your hard. Choose the one that pays off.

COMFORT TRAPS

The real threat to leadership today isn't failure, it's comfort.

Comfort sneaks in when things are going well and whispers, "You've made it." But the truth is, the higher you rise, the more you need to stay sharp.

I'm not saying make reckless decisions or max out credit cards for motivation. But I *am* saying stop looking for easy. COVID trained people to default to comfort: stay home, stream it, DoorDash it. But comfort is the enemy of growth. If you want to grow, you have to get uncomfortable again.

> Discipline is uncomfortable.
> Pressure is uncomfortable.
> Sacrifice is uncomfortable.
> But that's where success lives.

The way I see it, there are several "comfort traps" that leaders face, whether they're in the fitness business or any other industry.

1. PROMOTION

Too many leaders think that once they've earned the title, they've made it. They see the new position as a finish line instead of a starting point. But every promotion resets the clock. The expectations get higher. The team gets bigger. The pressure increases. Leadership isn't about arrival; it's about renewal. The moment you think you've made it, you're already on your way down.

2. COMPENSATION

Making more money can distort your mindset if you're not careful. Suddenly, the lifestyle expands with the paycheck, and the hunger that drove your early success starts to fade. The work that built your career begins to soften. Money should create opportunity, not complacency. Be smart with it; save, invest, reward yourself responsibly. But don't ever let it convince you that you've "made it." Because the moment comfort seeps into your work habits, performance starts to decline right behind it.

3. MARKETING DEPENDENCY

In our industry, we spend millions driving traffic into our clubs; and marketing is a great tool, but it's not a substitute for hustle. If your team is sitting around waiting for leads to walk in instead of being out in the community building relationships, generating referrals, and asking for business, they've already lost their edge. Marketing can open doors, but leadership still requires creating momentum at the ground level.

> "Don't wait for the phone to ring and the door to swing. Make it happen!"
>
> *–Jim Rowley*

4. INNOVATION ARROGANCE

I've seen this happen time and again. A company gets a few wins, catches the competition, and then stops pushing forward. Meanwhile, the true innovators keep moving, keep experimenting, and keep learning. Innovation isn't a milestone. It's a muscle. Stop working it, and it weakens fast.

> "For every gym I open, I remodel two."
>
> *—Vince Julien*

5. MENTAL STAGNATION

Leaders stop reading, stop asking questions, stop learning. They rely on experience instead of curiosity. The best leaders I know are still students. They're humble enough to know that growth never ends and tough enough to hold themselves accountable to keep evolving.

The antidote to comfort is **intentional discipline**.

Reset your hunger daily.

Get into the field.

Learn constantly.

Shop competitors and businesses that inspire you.

Lead from the front, not from the desk.

> "Success is a choice."
>
> *—Jim Rowley*

A culture of high standards isn't built on perfection; it's built on leaders who refuse to settle.

TOOL: THE CULTURE FILTER

Before you bring someone onto your team, run them through this:

- **Drama:** Do they shut it down or stir it up?
- **Energy:** Do they raise the room or drain it?
- **Humility:** Do they say "we" more than "me"?
- **Resilience:** Do they face challenges or fold?
- **Respect:** Do they treat people well—members, teammates, leaders?

If they fail even one, they fail the filter.

STORY: CLOSING CLUBS TO BUILD CULTURE

When we bought Crunch out of bankruptcy in 2009, there were thirty-six gyms open. On day one, we closed eight of them. Not because the people were bad, but because the culture was. Those locations were too far from the center, too unsupported, and too disconnected from what we needed to build.

They had equipment. They had talent. What they lacked was **standards**. They accepted excuses. And excuses destroy brands faster than competition ever will.

Closing those clubs sent a message: **We are going to build a culture defined by effort and accountability. No exceptions.**

If you're too afraid to demand high performance, you'll never build a winning team.

Culture isn't shaped by slogans or mission statements. It's shaped by behavior, especially the behavior leaders tolerate.

And here's the truth we don't like to say out loud: **Every team is a mirror.** A reflection of its leader's standards and consistency.

If you want a stronger team, you have to become a stronger mirror—one that reflects clarity instead of confusion, commitment instead of convenience, and standards instead of shortcuts.

EXERCISE: CULTURE STANDARDS AUDIT

1. List the last three times your team missed a goal.

   ____

   ____

   ____

2. Identify whether each miss was caused by lack of skill or lack of standards.
3. If it was standards, ask: *What did I tolerate?*
4. Write down three non-negotiable behaviors you will no longer allow.

   ____

   ____

   ____

5. Share them in your next team meeting and uphold them.

"Don't pray for comfort; pray for strength."
—Jim Rowley

CHAPTER 2 VERY IMPORTANT POINTS

- Culture is built on standards, not slogans.
- The moment you tolerate excuses, you forfeit excellence.
- High standards attract high performers; low standards invite drama.
- Discipline beats talent when talent gets soft.
- Comfort is the enemy; choose the hard that pays off.

Part II

BUILDING YOUR LEADERSHIP DNA

True leadership is built on character, intuition, and curiosity—valuing steadfastness and self-awareness over résumés, trusting your gut through preparation, and knowing enough about everything to connect the dots. It's your DNA, not your résumé.

Chapter 3

WHAT'S YOUR DEAL?

"Teams are not built from superstars alone. They are built from people who care about the collective win."

—Jim Rowley

When I interview someone for a role, I don't just want to know where they worked. I want to know *who they are.* Where did they grow up? What did their parents do? Were they a captain on their sports team, or were they the kid who rode the bench but showed up to every practice anyway?

I'll take the benchwarmer nine times out of ten. Why? Because DNA matters more than résumé. You can train skill sets, but you can't manufacture character.

Years ago, I was hiring for a management role. One candidate had an impressive résumé: big brands, polished experience, all the shiny credentials. The other had far less experience and told me he played high school football. He admitted he rarely got on the field, but he never missed a practice. He carried water, ran drills, and supported his teammates to the final whistle.

I hired the benchwarmer. He became one of the most consistent, humble, dependable leaders in the company.

That's DNA.

Too many leaders fall in love with credentials. They want the slick résumé, the Ivy League pedigree, the "rock star" candidate who knows how to talk the talk. But when the pressure hits, you don't need the showpiece. You need the grinder. You need the person whose DNA is built on humility, loyalty, perseverance, and a team-first mentality.

One of the most memorable things I've ever been part of was a TV pilot concept called *The Boss is Coming to Dinner*. On the surface, it sounds like a show. In reality, it was a completely different way of thinking about how you evaluate people.

Instead of having the candidate, polished résumé in hand, sit across the desk from the interviewer in an office, we flipped the entire process. We selected a group of candidates who were interviewing for a general manager role; and rather than bringing them into a conference room, we went to them. The interview happened in their home.

Each candidate hosted dinner.

That was the interview.

Now think about what that actually reveals. You are not seeing rehearsed answers or memorized talking points. You are seeing how someone lives, how they think, how they prepare, and how much they care about the details.

As I walked into each home, I was not just there to eat. I was observing everything. Cleanliness. Organization. Design choices. Attention to detail. You can tell a lot about a person by what they tolerate in their own environment.

Then you sit down for dinner, and another layer opens up.

What did they prepare?

Was there thought behind it?

Did they consider the guest experience?

Did they plan, or did they just throw something together?

Even small things told a story. I remember going to the restroom in one home and there were no hand towels. Nothing to dry your hands on. That might seem insignificant, but it is not. That is attention to detail. That is awareness. That is preparation. And those same traits show up in how someone leads a business.

Some dinners were clearly well thought out. Others felt rushed, almost like the person did not fully understand the opportunity in front of them. You could feel the difference immediately.

What made the experience powerful was that it was real. There was no script. No artificial setting. You were seeing the person in their natural environment, which is where the truth always shows up.

After going through multiple candidates, we narrowed it down to a final group. Then we reversed the process. I hosted them at my home. They met my family. They saw how I live. They had the chance to ask me questions, not just as a hiring manager, but as a person.

That part matters just as much.

This was not just about my evaluating them. It was about their evaluating me. It created a level of transparency and connection that you will never get sitting in an office going line by line through a resume.

In the end, one person was selected for the role. But the real takeaway was not just the outcome. It was the process.

Too many leaders rely on resumes and rehearsed interviews to make decisions about people. That only tells you what someone has done. It does not tell you who they are.

If you want to understand someone's DNA, you have to get outside of the traditional setting. You have to see how they think, how they operate, and how they show up when it is real.

That experience reinforced something I believe deeply: Great leaders do not just evaluate credentials. They evaluate character, awareness, and consistency.

Because at the end of the day, the little things are never little.

I've worked with world-class athletes and global icons. I co-founded UFC Gym. I helped build Hard Candy Fitness with Madonna. We launched a chain with Alex Rodriguez in Mexico. But the biggest lesson wasn't about fame or glamour; it was about consistency. The people who last, who lead, who elevate everyone around them are the ones with the right DNA.

As leaders, our job is to identify that DNA early and bet on it. Résumés can exaggerate. Skills can be overstated. But DNA shows up in how someone reacts to failure, how they treat the front-desk staff, and whether they finish what they start.

So when I ask a candidate, "What's your deal. How do you describe yourself?" I'm not looking for polished accomplishments. I'm looking for the blueprint behind the résumé. What drives you? What do you believe in? When things get hard, and they will, do you find a way, or do you fold?

When I'm in an interview, I'm not just listening to what someone says; they're telling me who they are long before they realize it. One of the biggest red flags for me is when a candidate, especially at the executive level, hasn't taken the time to truly understand what they're applying for. They haven't thought deeply about the role, the business, or the strategy. They show up without a plan, without perspective, and without purpose. That tells me a lot about how they lead.

Another tell is language. If I hear a lot of *"I did this"* and *"I achieved that"* but not a lot of *"we"* or *"the team,"* that's an immediate concern. Leadership isn't a solo sport; it's a team effort. We're a team-building organization; and if someone can't naturally speak in terms of collaboration and shared success, they won't fit our culture.

Preparation also matters. I can tell who's done their homework. The right candidate has visited multiple Crunch clubs, scoped out competitors, talked to members, and comes in with ideas. They don't just tell me what they've done; they show me how they think. They might say, "Here's something I noticed," or "Have you ever thought about approaching it this way?" That kind of curiosity and initiative is what separates the prepared from the complacent.

Then there's chemistry. I've learned over the years that if I wouldn't want to spend time with someone outside of work, I probably don't want to work with them every day. We spend too much time together for that connection not to matter. If there's something off, like an energy that doesn't align or a lack of authenticity, that's a red flag. If we can't connect one-on-one, it's going to be even tougher in a boardroom, on a call, or when they're leading a team under pressure. You can read every book, you can listen to every podcast, you can even be mentored and educated; but at some point, *you need to trust your instincts* about the people you hire.

And finally, one of the most telling signs of all: They don't show interest in the person sitting across from them. If you're interviewing to work for someone, you should be genuinely curious about them: their leadership style, their vision, their challenges. Ask, "What keeps you up at night?" "What are the biggest goals for your team right now?" or "How do you see competition shaping the next phase of the business?" Even a personal question, something like, "I read that you're a Marine; how does that experience shape how you lead?" shows engagement and emotional intelligence.

At the executive level, an interview isn't about impressing; it's about connecting. I want to see if you're thoughtful, if you're curious, if you're wired for problem-solving. I'll often ask, "Tell me about a time you faced what seemed like an impossible challenge. How did you overcome it?" If you've never faced real adversity, this probably isn't the right place for you. We operate in a high-performance culture that rewards resilience and creativity.

A résumé might get you in the room; but it's your DNA, your preparation, your humility, your energy, your curiosity, that determines whether you belong in the room.

Because the truth is, résumés fade. **DNA doesn't.**

And if you want to build a winning team, you have to become a student of DNA.

WHAT'S YOUR STORY?

Before the titles, before the accolades, before anyone knew my name, I was sitting in a cramped apartment in Sacramento with my back against the wall, literally and financially. Rent was $440 a month. My wife and I had no idea how we were going to pay it. With a Chevron credit card in hand, I wasn't thinking about gas; I was thinking about groceries. That card meant one thing: thirty days to figure it out.

So I hustled.
Thirty days of dialing from a windowless room.
Thirty days surrounded by White Pages and a rotary phone.
Thirty days of grinding for ten appointments a day.
No shortcuts. No safety net.

That was the moment. The pivot between fear and faith.

Truthfully, when I first started in this business, I went to the manager and tried to quit every payday. But she refused to let me leave. She continued to pour her time, effort, and energy into me, building my belief that this was something I really had a gift for. Every time, she encouraged me to stay and talked me out of quitting. Thank you Rose Olsen for believing in me.

I could've folded, and many did. But instead, I chose belief. Not in luck. In fortitude. In purpose. In showing up.

That Chevron moment wasn't a footnote; it was a forge. It became the story behind my story. Not one built on excuses, but on the decision to take ownership when it mattered most.

Because leadership doesn't come from résumé lines. Leadership comes from choosing faith when fear feels easier.

So let me ask you: **Is your story driven by fear or by faith?**

Too many people treat their past like a limitation:

"I didn't go to college."
"I grew up in a rough neighborhood."
"I didn't have anyone to guide me."

Those things are real. But here's the truth: **Everyone has a story.** The difference is whether you let your story define you or drive you. It's up to you to write, define, take charge of, and ultimately share your story. Part of the legacy that I've aspired to leave behind is an understanding that your unique experiences influence others. People want to be included in your life beyond your managerial skills and practices.

> "The biggest part of judging character is knowing yourself."
>
> *—Jim Rowley*

WHERE THE CLIMB BEGINS

Where the climb begins is where the fight begins. Every time you step into a new opportunity or earn a promotion, that's when the real battle starts; it's an internal one. The questions creep in: *Am I spending too much time on this? Am I neglecting that? Can I really handle this next level?* That's the fight: the push and pull between confidence and doubt, between drive and balance. It's not about proving yourself to others anymore; it's about managing the noise in your own head. Every leader faces it. The key is to recognize that the climb doesn't get easier; you just get stronger.

So when that one-shot opportunity shows up you can't afford to miss, what are you going to do with it? Too many people let their past talk them out of their future. They get the opportunity, and then they start doubting whether they belong. Most people don't fall because they lack talent, but because they let self-doubt creep in.

Your past shouldn't be an anchor. It should be your fuel.

One of the most successful franchisees in the Crunch system, Tony Hartl, grew up in St. Louis, raised by a single mom who was up at 4:30 every morning. That's where he started but not where he stayed. Today he's a model of what consistency and high standards can create. But don't just look at the version of Tony you see now; remember the kid from St. Louis who made a decision to shape his own story.

That same decision is in front of you right now.

TOOL: THE FIVE DNA MARKERS

1. **Humility** — Puts the team above self
2. **Perseverance** — Shows up even when it's difficult
3. **Loyalty** — Stays true in both good times and bad
4. **Coachability** — Seeks feedback and acts on it
5. **Finish Energy** — Completes what they start

When evaluating candidates or talent, score them on these five. Anyone can fake it for a day, but DNA reveals itself over time.

EXERCISE: DNA INTERVIEW

Next time you're hiring or even evaluating your current team, try this:

1. Ask each person to tell a story about a time they failed. Watch how they describe it. Do they blame others, or do they own it?
2. Ask them who influenced them most growing up. Look for gratitude, humility, and respect.
3. Ask about a time they finished something difficult when no one was watching.

The answers will reveal their DNA faster than any résumé ever will.

EXERCISE

Write down the top 10 impactful moments in your life that you'd be comfortable sharing with others:

1. ______________________________
2. ______________________________
3. ______________________________
4. ______________________________
5. ______________________________
6. ______________________________
7. ______________________________
8. ______________________________

9. ____

10. ____

"A résumé might get you in the room, but it's your DNA that determines whether you belong in the room."

–Jim Rowley

CHAPTER 3 VERY IMPORTANT POINTS

- DNA matters more than résumés; character outperforms credentials.
- Humility, loyalty, perseverance, and finish energy predict long-term success.
- Curiosity, preparation, and self-awareness reveal real leadership potential.
- Your story is fuel, not an anchor. Lead from what shaped you.
- Leaders win by betting on people whose habits match the mission.

CRUNCH

Chapter 4

TRUST YOUR GUT

"Most alpha leaders, those who become highly capable, live in a positive state. They live in an optimistic state because they've laid down the foundational work that allows them to be highly capable."

–Bonnie Watson Coleman

Data matters. Metrics matter. Scoreboards matter. But in leadership, there will always be moments when you don't have every fact, when the numbers don't tell the full story, and when hesitation costs you the win.

In those moments, you have to trust your gut.

Trusting your gut isn't about being reckless or ignoring reality. It's about developing the self-awareness and situational awareness to make decisions quickly, confidently, and in alignment with your values.

In the Marines, hesitation was dangerous. You learned to read the field, assess what you could, and act. Waiting for perfect information could cost lives. Business is different, but the principle holds: **If you wait for perfect clarity, you'll miss the opportunity.**

Too many leaders hide behind endless analysis: one more report, one more meeting, one more assurance. But what they're really doing is avoiding the responsibility of deciding. Leadership is about deciding.

Trusting your gut comes from preparation. It comes from laying the foundation of discipline, learning, and experience so that when your instincts fire, they're drawing on something real.

I train leaders using something I call the **Brown Bag Theory**. Everyone walks into work carrying a bag: personal stress, financial worries, relationship issues, and a thousand small problems. The mistake is bringing that bag inside.

If you want to be trusted as a leader, you need to **leave the bag at the door**.

When I walk into a club or a meeting, I imagine setting my bag down outside. My team doesn't need my distractions. They need presence, clarity, and confidence.

Trusting your gut is easier when you're not weighed down by everything you carried in with you.

I've trusted my gut to close clubs that weren't working, even when it wasn't popular. I've trusted my gut to back people others overlooked. I've trusted my gut to invest in ideas that didn't make sense on paper. Were they all right? No. But the willingness to act and to own the outcome is what separates capable leaders from highly capable ones.

If you want to grow as a leader, you must learn to hear that inner voice and act when it matters.

A leader I once worked for told me something I'll never forget: **"It's not always your job to have all the answers, but it *is* your job to know what questions to ask."** That line stuck with me because too many leaders think they must walk into every room as the expert. You don't. But you *do* need to be curious, connected, and confident enough to ask the questions that guide your people to the answers.

Take a franchise manager closing under 75 percent. Instead of rushing in to fix it yourself, ask:

> How are you opening your presentation?
> Where does it feel like the conversation loses momentum?
> What do you think you're missing?

Sit back. Listen. That's where the discovery happens. That's where real coaching begins. Great leaders guide. They don't rescue.

So stop putting pressure on yourself to be the answer machine. Start being the leader who unlocks answers through better questions.

TOOL: THE FOUR ASSESSMENTS

Before acting on your gut, run yourself through these quick checks:

1. **Self-Awareness** — *How do I feel right now? Am I grounded or reactive?*
2. **Self-Regulation** — *What can I do to shift my mindset or reset my state?*

DRIVE VS. DREAM

Everybody wants the win, but not everybody's willing to *work* for it. There's a big difference between dreaming and driving. Dreams are cheap. Drive is costly. I've always believed if you want something, you have to immerse yourself in it. Study it. Touch it. Smell it. Want a Porsche? Know the specs. Sit in one. Go test drive it. Want to build the best club? Get out of your own box and go visit the best. Sit in on their meetings. Ask questions. Learn what they're doing that you're not. Don't assume they've just got better equipment or better luck; find out. When I led regional sales, I rented a van and drove my team club to club with checklists in hand. Why? To shake things up. To open their eyes. To turn dreams into drive. Because wishing doesn't get it done. Action does. You want more? *Do more.* Be consumed with it. *Never hope for it more than you're willing to work for it.*

3. **Situational Awareness** — *How are others feeling? What's the emotional temperature of the room?*
4. **Situational Regulation** — *What can I influence right now to move things forward?*

These checks sharpen your instincts and keep your decisions aligned.

EXERCISE: THE GUT DRILL

This week, pick three decisions you've been delaying: big or small.

a. ______________________________

b. ______________________________

c. ______________________________

1. Limit yourself to five minutes of review for each.
2. Run through the four assessments quickly for each.
3. Make the call.
4. Record the result and reflect: Was your gut right? If not, what can you learn to refine it?

"At the end of the day, if you have the skillset, the understanding, and the opportunity, then it's up to you."

– Jim Rowley

CHAPTER 4 VERY IMPORTANT POINTS

- Perfect information never arrives; decisive leaders move anyway.
- Gut instinct is earned through discipline, reps, and self-awareness.
- Preparation sharpens intuition; hesitation dulls it.
- Asking the right questions is often more powerful than having the right answers.
- Confidence comes from clarity and presence, not bravado.

Chapter 5

KNOW A LITTLE ABOUT A LOT

"The magic you're looking for is in the work you're avoiding."
– Chris Williamson

Leadership isn't just about knowing your lane. It's about knowing enough about *all* the lanes to connect the dots, challenge assumptions, and make better decisions.

Too many managers hide inside their comfort zone:

"I'm a sales guy."
"I'm an ops person."
"I just run the front desk."

That mindset keeps you average. A leader who understands only one slice of the business is always at the mercy of someone else's expertise.

The best leaders **know a little about a lot**. They may not be the world's top accountant, but they understand the flow of the numbers. They may not be master trainers, but they can instantly tell whether a class is running well. They may not write the marketing campaigns, but they know enough to ask sharp, strategic questions.

One example that really shaped my perspective came from simply being out in the field, watching, asking questions, and staying curious. I used to visit competitors, attend fitness competitions, and observe how people were training. I noticed something subtle: Young women were carving out small spaces in clubs to do floor work. They'd grab dumbbells and a mat and find a corner to train. Over time, I saw this pattern everywhere.

That small observation turned into a massive industry shift. Back in the 1990s, we started designing open floor plans—what we now call turf sections. At first, it was just rubber flooring. Then it became turf. Then we added balls, bands, TRX straps, and all the tools for functional training. Today, almost every gym in the world has an open space like that. It started with curiosity, not certainty.

That's what "knowing a little about a lot" is really about. You don't have to have all the answers as a leader, but you do need to know which questions to ask. You gather feedback from data, from people, from what you observe; and that feedback helps you see trends early. Most people stop there. The real test of leadership is what you *do* with that insight. Can you take it, build a strategy around it, and lead people to execution through inspiration, motivation, and intellect to solve the problem or seize the opportunity?

Being curious doesn't just apply to innovation. It applies everywhere. Take something as simple as laundry in a gym. Most leaders never think about it. But ask a few questions: How long does it take to wash and fold towels? What's the utility cost? How much labor is tied up in that process? You don't have to be an expert in laundry to find ways to save money or improve efficiency. You just have to be curious enough to understand the function.

The same goes for sales. A lot of people avoid it because they think they're not "salespeople." But sales is really about curiosity and connection. The hard part isn't asking for money; it's building the value, the excitement, and the trust so that by the time you make the ask, the customer already feels it's the natural next step. If the ask feels hard, it's usually because the work leading up to it wasn't done well enough.

I don't sell memberships anymore, but I still consider myself a salesperson. Why? Because I've spent years honing those skills: learning how to listen, how to connect, and how to inspire action. And when you apply that mindset across disciplines—training, operations, member service, maintenance—you build a holistic understanding of how your business really works.

Too many leaders walk through their clubs or other businesses thinking only about their department. They skip the general knowledge that ties everything together. But the best leaders, the ones who see opportunities before everyone else, stay curious, stay informed, and stay connected to the full picture.

I've lived this truth. In the Marines, you had to understand not just your job but the job of the person next to you. In the fitness industry, every step, from 24 Hour Fitness to UFC Gym to Hard Candy Fitness to Crunch, forced me to broaden what I knew.

When we took Crunch out of bankruptcy, I didn't just look at sales. I had to understand facilities, finance, training, marketing, franchising, and private equity. If I had siloed myself, the brand would have stayed small. Instead, I forced myself to learn enough about each function to make the right calls and surround myself with the right experts. It wasn't glamorous. It was hours of listening, questioning, and digging into details outside my comfort zone. But it made me a stronger leader, and it gave me the confidence to trust my gut when the stakes were high.

Knowledge is leverage. When you understand the bigger picture, you move faster, think clearer, and lead more effectively.

And today, there's no excuse. You can learn the basics of almost anything in hours if you're hungry enough.

So if you want to lead at a higher level, stop saying, "That's not my area."

You don't need to be the expert. But if you know enough to ask smart questions, recognize patterns, and connect ideas, you'll always be one step ahead.

TOOL: THE T-MODEL LEADER

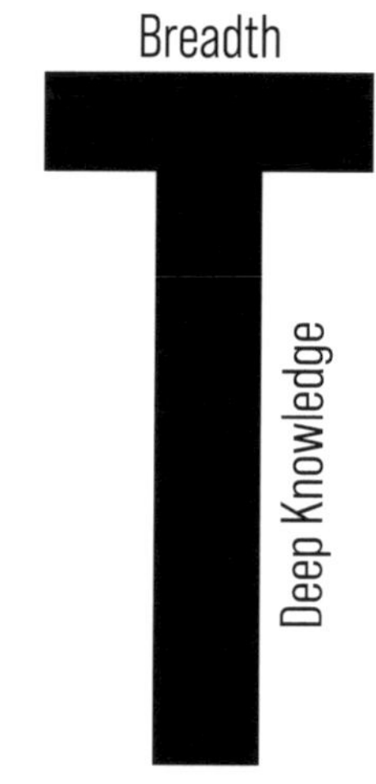

Picture the letter T.

- The **vertical stroke** is your deep area of expertise: the thing you know inside and out.
- The **horizontal stroke** is your breadth: the "little about a lot" knowledge that connects everything else.

Strong leaders are T-shaped. They go deep where they must, but they also go wide enough to understand, connect, and challenge across disciplines.

To be successful and highly effective in your teamwork responsibilities, you will need to know about and exercise both leadership and management behaviors. For example:

Teamwork	
Leadership and Management Behaviors	
Leadership	**Management**
Flexing your style to meet the needs of your team's development level	Use the guidelines for the stages of team development.
Recruit, train, and develop team members who have diverse backgrounds to strengthen the team and store results.	Remove obstacles as your team develops through the different stages.
Educate and communicate the value of teamwork.	Follow up on team goals and results.

The chart below shows the difference between the 20th century leadership mindset and the 21st century mindset. (I was raised on the 20th century mindset.)

21_{th} CENTURY LEADERSHIP

Late 20th Century Definition of Leadership: I get others to do what is needed by my authority. I have impact and make things happen.	**21st Century Definition of Leadership:** I create the conditions that motivate everyone to achieve Organizational goals. Things happen through others.
Mindsets:	
I Know	**They Know**
I tell them what to do and think	I set goals and teach them how to think
It's up to them (their future is their failure)	It's up to us (their failure us my failure)
I manage their actions	I create the conditions for them to be successful
I build relationships so people will do what I want	I am authentic and genuine in my relationships
If they aren't getting my message, they aren't listening	If they aren't getting my message, I'm not communicating effectively
Results In:	
Short-term efficiency gains	Long-term organizational improvements
Dis-empowerment	Empowerment
Obedience	Self-motivation
Resignation	Inspiration
Fear	Pride

The Trium Group

EXERCISE: BREADTH BUILDER

1. Make a list of five areas of the business you "don't know much about."

   a. ______________________________

   ____

   b. ______________________________

   ____

   c. ______________________________

   ____

   d. ______________________________

   ____

   e. ______________________________

   ____

2. For each, schedule one hour this month to learn: shadow a colleague, read an article, listen to a podcast, or sit with your numbers team.
3. At the end of the month, write down one insight from each area that changes how you think about leadership.
4. Share one of those insights with your team.

"Know a little about a lot, and you'll never be blindsided. Know only your lane, and you'll always be vulnerable."

– Jim Rowley

CHAPTER 5 VERY IMPORTANT POINTS

- Leaders must understand every lane enough to connect the dots.
- Curiosity drives innovation; comfort breeds blind spots.
- Field time reveals truths reports never will.
- Patterns and micro-observations fuel big breakthroughs.
- Knowledge across functions accelerates smarter, faster decisions.

Part III

LEADING PEOPLE AND DRIVING RESULTS

High-performing organizations are made by leaders who develop capable teams, enforce accountability, set non-negotiable standards, and elevate everyday people into consistent winners through systems and coaching. (Our goal as leaders is to get extraordinary results from everyday people.)

Chapter 6

YOU'RE ONLY AS GOOD AS YOUR TEAM

"There are three kinds of teams: incapable, capable, and highly capable. The incapable make excuses. The capable win sometimes. The highly capable win like dynasties."

– Peter Drucker

Leadership is a multiplier. You can be the most talented leader in the world; but if your team is weak, you'll never reach your potential. Flip it around: You can be an average leader, but if your team is highly capable, you'll look like a genius.

The Marines drove this truth home for me. Out in the field, your life depends on the men and women next to you. If they're prepared, disciplined, and locked into the mission, you can survive anything. If they're sloppy or self-centered, you're in danger. The business world is no different.

I break teams into three categories:

1. **Incapable Teams** — They make excuses, point fingers, avoid accountability, and hope someone else will solve the problem. Results are random, morale is low, and culture is toxic.
2. **Capable Teams** — They do *fine*. They hit goals sometimes. They win six months out of twelve. People call them "solid"; but really, they're average.
3. **Highly Capable Teams** — They win consistently. They don't rise and fall with circumstances; they deliver. These are your dynasties.

As a leader, your job isn't to maintain a capable team. It's to **build a highly capable one**. "Good enough" might get you through a season, but it won't build anything that lasts.

At Crunch, we've seen this across hundreds of clubs. Two locations can be in the same market with the same tools, same marketing, same brand. One thrives, one struggles. The difference is never the zip code. It's the **team**. A highly capable team is the greatest competitive advantage any leader can create.

But building a dynasty team takes intention. It means hiring people whose character and habits match the culture you want, not just people with polished résumés. It means consistent coaching and development. It means holding the line on standards and making tough calls quickly when someone isn't meeting the bar. It means celebrating wins without letting complacency sneak in.

The day you settle for "capable" is the day you begin to decline.

People often think scaling from two clubs to thousands requires some magical transformation. It doesn't. The fundamentals are the same. Managing a few is no different than managing many when your strategy is clear, your systems are strong, and your standards are non-negotiable. If you hire well, coach intentionally, build real relationships, show empathy, plan with precision, and enforce performance, then scale simply amplifies what already works.

Everyone gets nervous about taking on more. But scaling isn't about adding complexity, it's about **duplicating excellence**. You're not managing 400 different clubs; you're repeating the same proven execution 400 times. That's how you build teams that last and a business that endures.

TEAM LEADERSHIP AND DEVELOPMENT

One of the most effective leadership philosophies I've come across comes from Warren Buffett, one of the most successful businessmen in the world. He advises:

> "Surround yourself with people who push you to do and be better. No drama or negativity. Just higher goals and higher motivation. Good times and positive energy. No jealousy or hate. Simply bringing out the absolute best in each other."

I refer to this as the *ideal state:* the benchmark for how we should build and lead our teams. Whether in your personal or professional life, there's no greater aim than creating a culture rooted in this mindset. No one seeks the opposite. If you're leading a gym, a district, a region, or a personal training team, this is the target: Surround yourself with the kind of people who bring this ideal to life.

BUILDING THE RIGHT TEAM

Reaching this ideal state starts long before you ever discuss training, sales, revenue, or growth. It begins with **building the right team**, one person, one hire, one standard at a time.

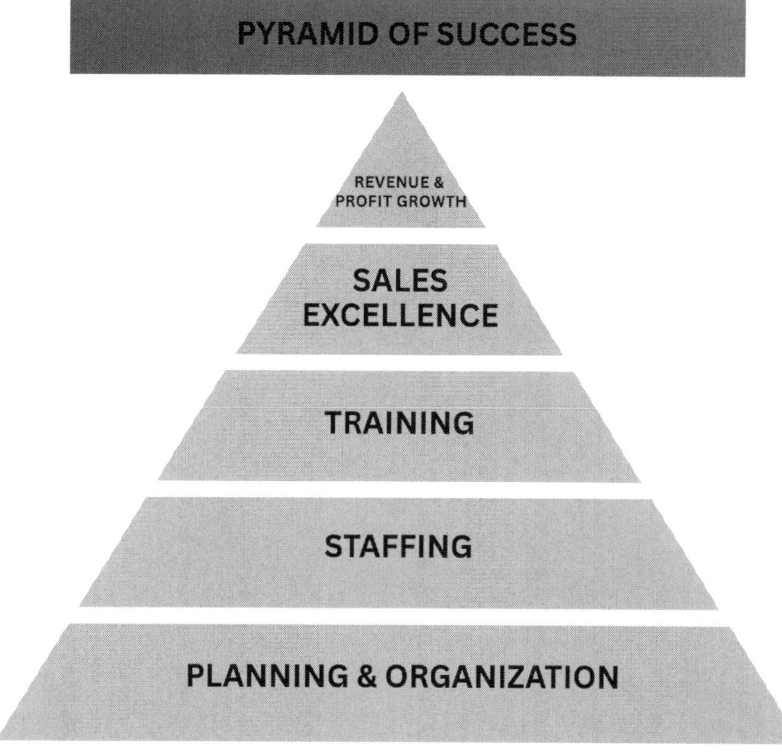

This foundational pyramid, common to every high-performing business, rests on three essentials:

- **A strong plan**
- **A strong team**
- **Proper training**

At the base is **planning**. Without a clear strategy and structure, even the most talented team will struggle. But once the plan is defined, everything rises or falls on the people responsible for executing it. Your team is your most valuable asset, and building it must be intentional not accidental.

> "Set your goals and aspirations, have a plan, and lock in."
> *– Jim Rowley*

The strongest team members share common traits. They:

- show up present and focused;
- are highly coachable;
- elevate the people around them;
- pursue growth consistently;
- over-deliver as a habit, not a surprise;
- follow through and finish what they start;
- respect their role and understand its impact;
- demonstrate humility and professionalism;

- take ownership of their responsibilities;
- stay curious and keep learning; and
- maintain a positive, constructive attitude.

These traits aren't "nice-to-haves"; they're necessary for high performance. When you fill your roster with people who embody them, the plan becomes easier to execute, training becomes more effective, and your results become predictable.

Let me pull back the curtain on how we operate.

There are four anchors that drive everything we do at the corporate level, and they apply just as much to a club manager as they do to a CEO:

1. **Strategy and Tactics** — What's the mission? What's the game plan? Do we know where we're going and why?
2. **Structure** — Is the organization built to execute that plan? Are roles clear, tools in place, and communication flowing?
3. **Talent** — Do we have the right people, and are they in the right seats?
4. **Measurement** — Can we track the results and prove the plan is working?

It's simple, but never easy. And it only works when we enforce two disciplines with extreme rigor: **Relentless Alignment** and **Ruthless Prioritization**.

Let's break that down.

Relentless Alignment means this: We don't hold meetings to fill calendars or kill time. We meet to align. We don't do hour-long PowerPoints. We don't chase rabbit holes. We talk strategy. We talk targets. We talk about how each piece fits into the bigger puzzle. When I say "relentless," I mean it. Every team session, every leadership huddle, every quarterly offsite is all about getting synced. If your team isn't aligned, they're guessing. And you can't afford guesswork when you're chasing high performance.

Ruthless Prioritization is the second key. I remember one strategy session where we had 73 "important" initiatives on the board. Seventy-three. You know how many we can actually execute at a high level in a year? Maybe five. So we boiled them down. We argued. We cut. We re-ranked. And we walked out with 15 priorities, and from there we narrowed to our top five. That's what great teams do. They get clear on what matters most and focus like crazy.

Here's the truth: If you're leading without prioritization, your team sees it. If you chase every shiny object or shift gears weekly, they won't follow with energy; they'll just try to survive the chaos. But if you lead with focus, they'll lock in, too.

If you want to scale your impact, start here:

- Revisit your strategy often; keep it sharp.
- Strengthen your structure so it supports execution.
- Relentlessly invest in talent. It's your only true long-term advantage.
- Align constantly by measuring results and course-correcting fast.
- Prioritize ruthlessly and eliminate noise.

That's how great teams—and dynasties—are built.

Years ago, when I was a general manager building a new sales team, I hired five sharp, driven people who were hungry to learn and ready to work. My job wasn't just to hit numbers; it was to lead them, develop them, and help them grow.

We didn't just hit our goals. We dominated. Month after month, we were the top-performing team. But the real accomplishment came later.

Over time, **three of those five team members became general managers themselves.** Shout-out to Michelle, Monica, and Reggie.

Think about that. Not only did we win in the moment, we also created a pipeline of future leaders. That's the mark of a strong team culture: results on paper *and* growth that outlasts your direct influence.

And that's one of the hardest truths about leadership: When you develop great people, they don't stay forever.

They get promoted.
They get noticed.
They get opportunities.

And as much as it stings to lose top performers, that's how you know you're doing it right.

It also means you must get good at recruiting, interviewing, training, rebuilding chemistry, and reestablishing culture over and over again. That's where real leadership shows itself: in how consistently you can replicate success.

If you want to get promoted yourself, you must be able to **export talent**, not hoard it. Leaders who hoard talent might win short-term, but they cap their ceiling. The best leaders build teams that function at a high level without constant direction and then let those people fly.

High performers need less supervision, but they generate more opportunity. That's the trade-off. And it's a trade-off you should welcome.

In the end, you're only as good as your team. And if your team keeps rising, it's the clearest sign you're leading the right way.

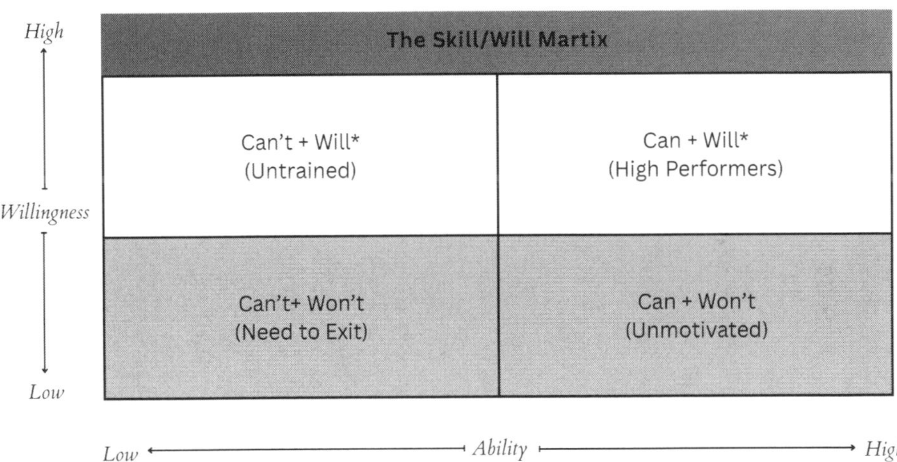

This is one of the core management tools we use at Crunch. We get very clear about which quadrant each person on the team is in; then we either build a specific plan to help them grow or make a decision about their long-term fit with the organization.

TOOL: THE TEAM DIAGNOSTIC

Ask yourself: *Do I lead a dynasty-caliber team, or just a "pretty good" one?*

Measure your team across five factors:

1. **Clarity** — Does every person know the mission, the metrics, and their role?
2. **Capability** — Do they have the skills and training to deliver?
3. **Character** — Do they demonstrate grit, humility, and loyalty?
4. **Chemistry** — Do they trust each other and pull in the same direction?
5. **Consistency** — Do they perform month after month, not just occasionally?

A dynasty-level team scores high in all five. Anything less needs immediate attention.

EXERCISE: TEAM REPORT CARD

Grade your current team A–F across the five Team Diagnostic categories:

- Any **C or below** is a risk to your results.
- Choose **one action this week** to raise each weak grade.
- Share the report card with your leadership team and **own the fixes together**.

"Learning who not to pick is more important than learning who to pick."

—Jim Rowley

CHAPTER 6 VERY IMPORTANT POINTS

- Teams determine your ceiling; leaders who build dynasties never settle for capable.
- Strategy, structure, and talent create predictable performance.
- Relentless alignment prevents drift.
- Ruthless prioritization keeps teams focused on what actually moves the needle.
- The strongest leaders export talent. They don't hoard it.

CRUNCH

Chapter 7

HOW TO MAKE EVERYDAY PEOPLE GET EXTRAORDINARY RESULTS

"Most people aren't superstars; but with the right systems and standards, you can take everyday people and build winning teams."

– Jim Rowley

Most of the people who work for you will not be all-stars. That's not a criticism. It's reality. The real question is: **What kind of leader are you going to be?** Are you going to complain about the talent you don't have, or are you going to build a system that gets extraordinary results from everyday people?

Great leaders are multipliers. They don't sit around waiting for superstars to walk through the door. They take the team they have and elevate it. They coach. They train. They build structures and systems that raise everyone's performance.

I've seen this play out in our clubs for decades. A front-desk team member who looked ordinary on paper became one of our top managers. A trainer who lacked confidence became a top performer after receiving guidance and encouragement. These transformations don't happen by accident. They happen because someone invested in them, coached them, developed them, and because the system made it possible. Investing in your team is not a nice-to-have; it is one of the highest-return decisions you will ever make as a leader.

Here's the story about the front-desk employee who was promoted to manager. On paper, she wasn't ready. She had no real leadership experience and didn't look like a future all-star.

But her DNA was strong.
She was loyal.
She was humble.
She was eager to learn.

So they invested in her with training, mentorship, repetition, and real accountability. Over time, she became one of the highest-performing managers in the entire region.

She didn't magically turn into a superstar. **The system elevated her. The culture lifted her. The leadership developed her.**

That's what great leaders do: They spot the spark, then teach people how to turn it into a fire.

Capability isn't fixed. People rise or fall depending on the environment you build.

If you establish a culture of accountability, growth, and recognition, even average team members will surprise you. If you allow excuses, inconsistency, and mediocrity, even talented people will underperform.

The key is simple: **Set clear standards and coach people to reach them.** That means transparent scoreboards, real-time feedback, and visible celebration of progress.

A big part of that environment is how you recognize and reward people. As you build these teams, you cannot skip the celebration piece. Publicly call out wins. Highlight the people who are doing what you are asking at a high level in local meetings, district meetings, company-wide meetings. Use incentives, bonuses, and simple shout-outs that show you see their effort and results.

What I've seen over and over again is that many people value genuine recognition as much as, and often more than, money. They want to know their work is respected and appreciated. When you consistently recognize those who are executing with high proficiency, you reinforce the behaviors you want and you send a clear message: This is a place where great work gets noticed.

And there's more to the idea of setting standards and coaching to them. It includes making your workplace a place where growth is expected and supported. Part of that growth comes from using the tools already built to help you succeed. One of our biggest advantages is our training ecosystem, like Crunch

University. Decades of proven systems, playbooks, videos, and step-by-step guidance. Leaders don't have to reinvent the wheel. The ones who win are the ones who master what already works.

Plug into the system.
Use the tools.
Execute.

That's how you multiply performance.

The myth is that results come from the "talented few." The reality is that most results come from the **middle of the team**. If you raise the middle, you win.

THE POWER OF FLOW

You have to teach your teams to *create* their own flow state. It doesn't just show up on its own.

For me, it starts with **focus**. When I'm focused, everything sharpens. My mind quiets down, the noise fades, and I can lock in on what really matters. I'm not chasing distractions or reacting to every little thing that comes flying at me. I'm intentional. I'm present.

And when I'm focused, I can tap into **resilience,** which is that inner drive that keeps me steady when things get hard. Resilience is what lets me push through the negativity, the setbacks, and the criticism that come with leadership. It's not about avoiding challenges; it's about facing them with strength and composure. I recognize when that negative bias starts creeping in, and I choose to rise above it. Resilience keeps me balanced. It keeps me moving forward.

When I combine focus and resilience, I can show up fully. I'm **present**. I'm right here: attentive, grounded, in the moment. Whether I'm talking with a team member, a colleague, or one of our members, I'm all in. That presence is powerful. People can feel it.

Then comes **confidence**. I walk tall knowing our company and leadership team have entrusted me with responsibility to lead, to coach, to develop others, and to grow our mission. I don't take that lightly. I carry that confidence with pride and humility. I don't look down as a leader. I keep my chin up, steady and strong.

And through it all, I stay **grateful**. Grateful for the opportunity to lead and to work in an industry that helps people live healthier, stronger, better lives. I get to make a difference every single day. That's something to be thankful for.

When I bring all those things together (focus, resilience, presence, confidence, and gratitude), I find my **flow state**. And when I'm in that state, I'm at my best. I'm unstoppable. The negativity can't stick. The distractions can't pull me away. I'm locked in.

But when I lose that gratitude, when my confidence dips, or when I let distractions pull me out of the moment, that's when it all unravels. That's when the worry, the doubt, the frustration start creeping in.

That's why every leader and team member needs to **define their own flow state**. What does it look like for you? How do you get there? Because just showing up, doing the same thing every day, hoping for better results, that's not leadership. That's maintenance.

CREATE A FLOW STATE

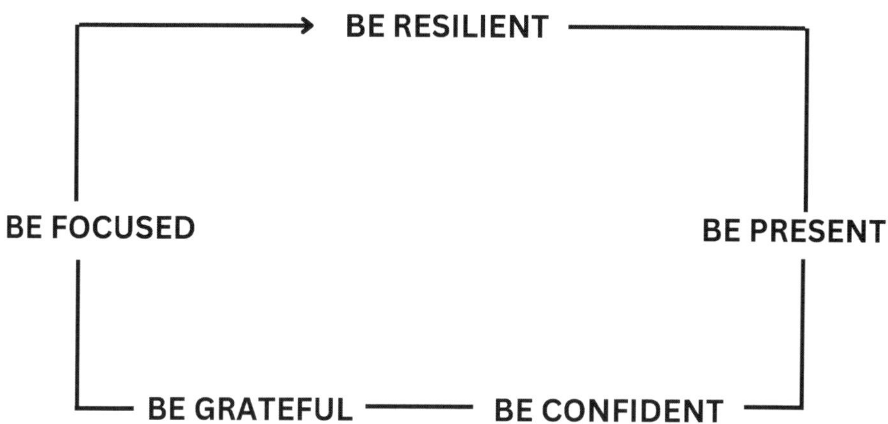

Leaders grow. Leaders change the environment. They make hard calls, take ownership, and push for progress, even when it's uncomfortable. That's what it takes to win. It's not supposed to be easy. That's why it's called work. But the rewards of seeing your team grow, seeing people win, feeling that sense of fulfillment are worth every ounce of effort.

When you stay focused, resilient, present, confident, and grateful, you hit your flow; and once you're there, you become unshakable. And when your team members hit flow, that's when you start to get extraordinary results from everyday people.

THE 4 E'S OF GREAT LEADERS (FROM JACK WELCH)

According to Jack Welch, legendary CEO of GE, outstanding leaders embody four critical traits:

1. **Energy** – They show up daily with purpose and drive.
2. **Energize** – They know how to motivate others and rally teams around a vision.
3. **Edge** – They're competitive and courageous in making tough decisions.
4. **Execute** – They deliver measurable results, understanding that productivity, not activity, is what matters.

While the concept for building a high-performing team is simple, execution is challenging. Here's how to do it right:

- **Be 100 percent involved** in every part of the process: recruiting, interviewing, hiring, onboarding, scheduling, and follow-through.
  - If you delegate this without oversight, you're trusting others to meet standards you haven't clearly defined.
- **Build a team, not a collection of individuals.** Invest in building talent pools.
- **Unify your team** with a shared mission and purpose.
- **Recognize and reward publicly.** Engage and praise regularly.
- **Stay engaged.** Watch, listen, and learn.
- **Support your team.** Respond to their needs with action.

I've mentioned this before, but it is so important that it bears repeating: To develop your team with consistency and impact, apply what I call the *Coaching Loop*:

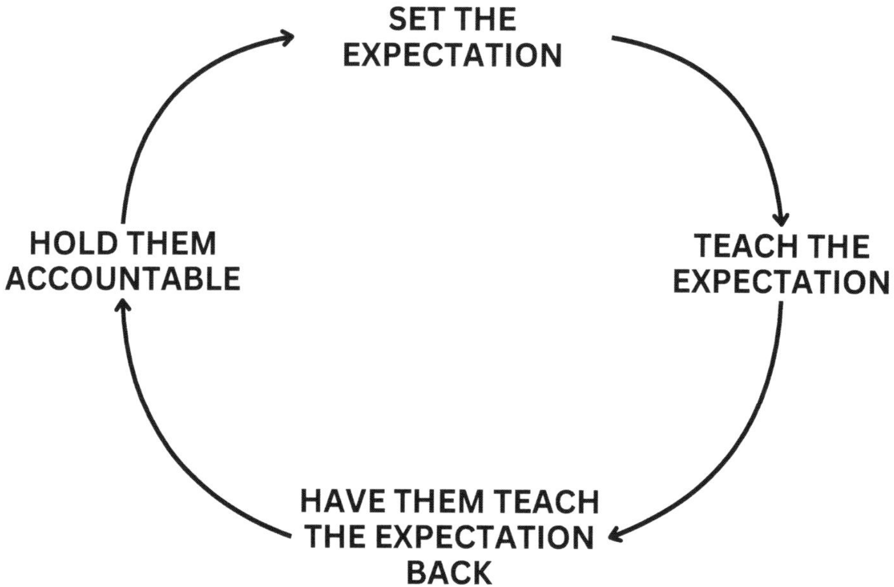

For example, if the expectation for a manager in our business is to sell 300 memberships this month, ask:

- Have they been trained to do that?
- Can they demonstrate back to you exactly how they will do it?

That *train-it-back* step is non-negotiable. It ensures they not only understand the "what" but also the "how." Then, close the loop with accountability.

If you're asking people to do something, make sure:

- you've trained them to do it; and
- you're willing to do it yourself if needed.

This is what leadership looks like.

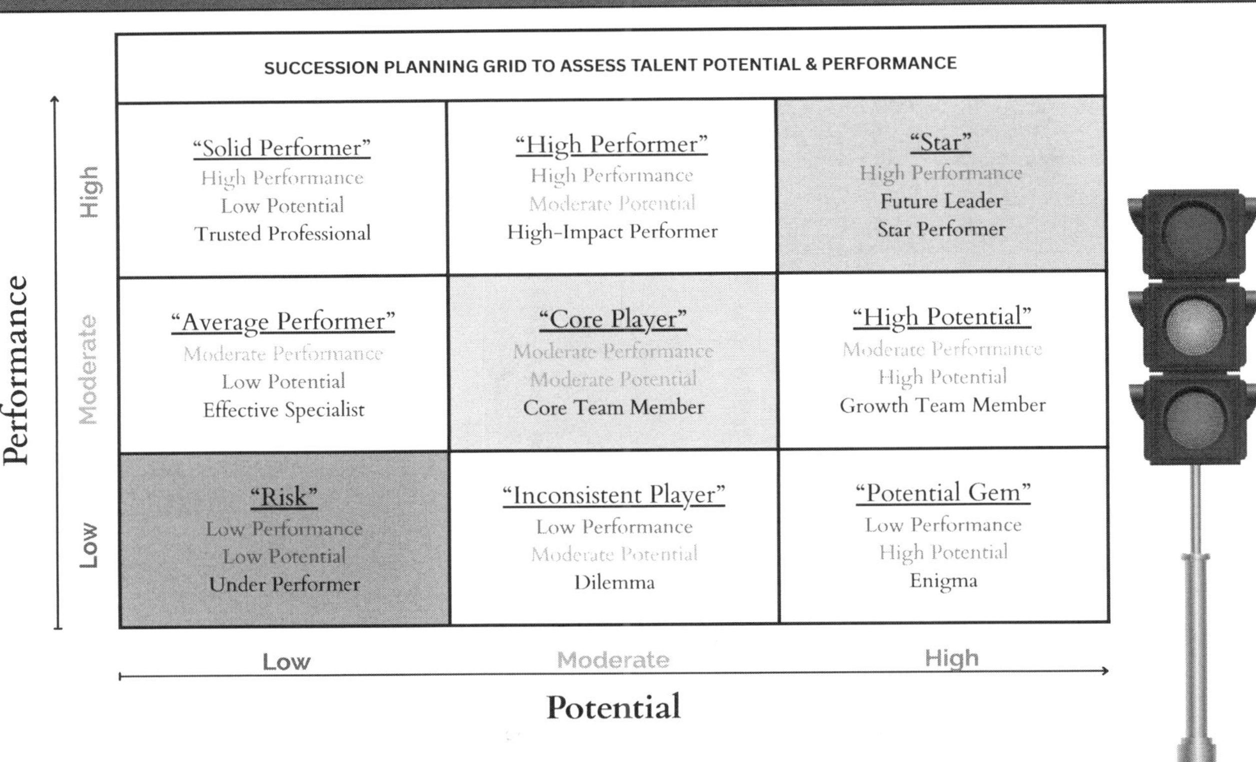

Credited to McKinsey & Company.

This is another management tool we use at Crunch. This nine-box tool helps you assess every person on your team through two lenses: performance and potential. Use the X and Y axes to plot each team member into the box that best reflects where they are today.

It is only effective if you are genuinely committed to coaching, retaining, and elevating your people. As a manager or leader, you have to slow down, think carefully about where each person truly belongs, and then use what you see here to drive your development plans, succession decisions, and overall team performance.

Building a strong internal talent pipeline is not optional; it's essential. We prefer to promote from within. If we consistently have to hire outside the organization to fill key roles, that's a red flag and it means we're not developing our own people.

> **Here's the truth every leader needs to swallow:**
> **Extraordinary teams aren't found. They're built.**
> Your systems build them.
> Your standards shape them.
> Your coaching elevates them.
> Your presence fuels them.

When you commit to developing everyday people into extraordinary performers, you're not just improving results, **you're changing lives.** You're giving people confidence they didn't know they had; opportunities they never imagined; and the belief that they can do more, be more, and achieve more.

And when your entire team starts operating with focus, resilience, presence, confidence, and gratitude, when they each find their flow, everything changes. Your culture strengthens.

Your performance surges. Your bench deepens. Your wins multiply.

Most leaders hope for talent. **Great leaders create it.**

If you want to build a dynasty, stop searching for superstars and start developing them. Build the environment. Build the expectations. Build the systems. Build the people. Because the day you decide that "ordinary" is good enough is the day your results become ordinary.

That's the work. That's the mission. And that's how you win every time.

Evaluate each person. Everyday people can become above-average performers by improving even one or two key traits.

"Capable teams hit their goals half the time. Highly capable teams hit their goals every time. The difference is leadership."

—Jim Rowley

CHAPTER 7 VERY IMPORTANT POINTS

- Systems, coaching, and standards elevate average people into consistent performers.
- Clear expectations, real scoreboards, and accountability produce predictable wins.
- The Coaching Loop is non-negotiable for skill development.

- Flow state matters. Focus, resilience, presence, confidence, and gratitude drive performance.
- Leaders create environments where growth is expected and supported.

Chapter 8

THE NUMBERS DON'T LIE: ACCOUNTABILITY

"People can argue with opinions, but they can't argue with the numbers. The numbers don't lie."

– Jim Rowley

Excuses are easy. Stories can be spun. Feelings can be manipulated. But numbers cut through all of it. The numbers don't lie, and they will always tell you the truth about your business.

"Facts over feelings."
- Jim Rowley

Accountability isn't about being harsh or punitive. It's about clarity. When the numbers are visible, everyone knows the standard. Everyone knows where they stand. And everyone knows whether they're winning or not.

At Crunch, we track everything that matters: sales, PT sessions, renewals, collections. These aren't just data points. They are accountability markers. A strong leader doesn't hide from them; they lean into them. They use them to coach, to motivate, to celebrate, and to correct.

And here's the part most leaders miss: **The moment you stop measuring, your team stops caring.** The moment you stop inspecting, standards start slipping. The moment you let "almost" be acceptable, excellence dies. They become medicore or average because leadership allowed that to be the standard.

Looking at numbers isn't enough; you have to act on them. Accountability starts with understanding the data, but it doesn't end there. You have to analyze trends, identify what's off track, and turn gaps into training opportunities. Too many managers glance at KPIs without forming a real plan. Let's say one of our Crunch franchisee's close rate is 15 percent below the standard. That's not just a stat; it's a red flag, and it calls for immediate corrective action. They would have to use the tools they have, like Crunch University, to build a targeted training plan. Then they would need to go right back to the fundamentals: **Set the expectation. Train to it. Have them train it back. Hold them accountable.** That's the loop. That's how you move the needle. Remember. **you can't manage what you don't measure**, and if you're not taking action on the numbers, you're not leading.

Weak leaders tell stories: "The market is tough." "Competition is heavy." "We're working hard." Strong leaders tell the truth: "We're at 80 percent of goal. Here's how we close the gap."

Someone once asked me how I get leaders to push past that "close enough" mentality, when people think hitting 80 percent of the target is good enough. My first reaction is simple: *Who wants to be average?*

Nobody shows up on day one aiming to be mediocre. People want to win. They want to be part of something that matters. But the difference between teams that *say* they want to win and those that *actually do* comes down to leadership (specifically, how you hire, coach, develop, and hold people accountable).

When COVID hit, our industry was in crisis. Clubs closed overnight. Revenue collapsed. Fear spread faster than facts. The leaders who survived weren't the ones with the biggest budgets. They were the ones who tracked the numbers relentlessly: cash flow, digital engagement, membership freezes, reopening metrics. Some leaders panicked and froze. Others leaned into accountability. They measured, adapted, and made tough calls quickly. Those are the leaders who lived to fight another day. That's not to say it was easy; it wasn't. But it wasn't impossible.

It was a brutal lesson, but a powerful one; the numbers don't lie, and the leaders who embrace them win, even in crisis.

If you bring in individuals who are content with 80 percent effort, that's the culture you'll get. But if you surround yourself with people who crave excellence, who take pride in outperforming expectations, then accountability becomes natural; it's built into the DNA of the team.

The truth is, average results don't last long. Over time, average gets you replaced. If management won't change, you change management. Every organization that wants to grow is looking for above-average performance; and if you're leading a team, your energy has to set that tone. You have to bring enthusiasm, intensity, and drive every day.

Apathy kills performance. If you're the kind of leader who's okay with "good enough," how can you expect your team to chase great? You can't inspire, motivate, or coach people if you don't model the standard yourself. Accountability isn't just about calling people out; it's about calling them *up*.

When your team sees that you're committed to training, developing, and pushing for that extra 20 percent, they'll follow your lead. The ones who don't will eventually weed themselves out. That's the reality of a performance-driven culture: It rewards effort, energy, and ownership.

In the end, accountability isn't punishment; it's alignment. It's making sure everyone's chasing the same vision with the same intensity. And when that happens, 100 percent stops being the exception. It becomes the expectation.

So don't hide from the numbers.
Don't soften them.
Don't apologize for them.

Put them on the wall.
Put them in the meetings.
Put them in the conversations.

Let them drive clarity.
Let them drive urgency.
Let them drive excellence.

In the Marines, accountability was life or death. You didn't just say your unit was ready; you checked weapons, inspected gear, counted rations. You verified. In business, it may not be life or death, but it's survival. Inspect what you expect. Because in the end **the numbers don't lie, and neither does your performance.** If you're brave enough to face the scoreboard every day, your team will follow you anywhere.

That's how great leaders win. That's how great cultures are built. And that's how you turn accountability into your greatest competitive advantage.

EXERCISE: LIFT THE MIDDLE

1. **Pick three "average" performers** on your team.
2. **Identify their weakest "E"** from Jack Welch's 4 E's: Energy, Energize, Edge, or Execute.
3. **Choose one targeted action** this week (training, coaching, feedback, or recognition) to lift that trait.
4. **Review progress in thirty days** and repeat the cycle.

EXERCISE: BUILD YOUR SCOREBOARD

1. Identify the five numbers that drive your business.
2. Make them visible to your entire team. Post them where everyone can see.

3. Review them weekly with your leadership team.
4. Hold one conversation this week where you use the numbers to coach, not just give opinions.

Accountability isn't a punishment. It's the foundation of performance.

"Inspect what you expect.
If you don't measure it, you can't lead it."
—Jim Rowley

CHAPTER 8 VERY IMPORTANT POINTS

- Clarity comes from metrics; what gets measured drives performance.
- Accountability aligns teams and fuels a culture of ownership.
- Great leaders act on data, not excuses; inspection precedes correction.
- Excellence dies where mediocrity is accepted; reject "close enough."
- Your standards shape your culture; model urgency, drive, and intensity.

Chapter 9

IT'S NOT WHAT YOU PREACH, IT'S WHAT YOU TOLERATE

"You don't get the culture you preach.
You get the culture you tolerate."
– Jim Rowley

Every leader has a vision. They talk about culture. They preach values. They put mission statements on the wall. But here's the truth: You don't get the culture you talk about. You get the culture you tolerate.

That idea first clicked for me years ago when I heard the quote I mentioned earlier from Kiko Suarez, a Navy SEAL: *"It's not what you preach, it's what you tolerate."* I latched onto that more than a decade ago, and it's stuck with me ever since.

If you allow excuses, you'll have an excuse-driven team. If you let gossip slide, you'll have a toxic culture. If you ignore mediocrity, you'll end up with a mediocre business.

People pay far more attention to what you accept than to what you say. The moment you let someone slide on being late, or cutting corners, or missing a goal without consequence, you've sent a message to everyone else: "This behavior is okay here."

In the Marines, standards weren't suggestions. If your uniform wasn't right, you fixed it. If your gear wasn't squared away, you corrected it. If you missed a step, someone called you out on the spot. That consistency built trust. Everyone knew the standard was real because it was enforced every time.

In business, too many leaders avoid hard conversations. They let things slide because they don't want conflict. But the cost of avoiding conflict is culture erosion. Every time you tolerate a behavior that doesn't match your standard, you weaken the entire team.

At Crunch, we've built a culture around accountability, energy, and positivity. But that didn't happen by preaching it into existence. It happened by drawing lines, enforcing standards, refusing to compromise, and letting some people go and firing others. Leaders at every level know: What you tolerate is what you teach.

Every standard you enforce strengthens your culture. Every standard you ignore weakens it. There is no neutral. You are either building culture or eroding it, every single day.

I often describe three kinds of mindsets that show up in teams:

- **Responsibility Mindset**
  - These individuals inspire action, unlock breakthroughs, and drive innovation.
  - They take ownership and explore possibilities to improve outcomes.
- **Victim Mindset**
  - These are the complainers, the resistors, and the blamers.
  - They seek validation and often create toxic alignment through negativity and sabotage.
- **Do-Nothing Mindset**
  - These individuals avoid conflict and responsibilities.
  - They sit idle, placating others without contributing meaningful value.

Left unchecked, the victim and do-nothing mindsets spread like weeds. If you tolerate them, they multiply. The only way to build a responsibility-driven culture is to weed out the other two. That takes courage, but it's non-negotiable. One franchisee once told me, "I don't know why my team isn't performing. I keep telling them what I expect." My response: "It's not about what you expect. It's about what you allow." Once he stopped letting lateness, weak effort, and negativity slide, his culture changed almost overnight.

If your team is filled with victims or passive participants, hitting goals will be a constant struggle. Your goal should be to build a team filled with individuals who embody a **responsibility mindset;** these are people who believe *Every situation I'm in is shaped, at least in part, by my actions, my inactions, or my interpretations. I always have the power to affect the outcome.*

There is no greater priority for a manager than this: **Identify, recruit, hire, and develop talent.**

Get the right people in the right seats doing the right things. When that alignment happens, results follow. Always seek the *perfect fit*, not just the perfect résumé.

"Responsibility, Victim, or Do-Nothing.
Every team member is one of the three.
Your culture depends on which one you tolerate."
– Jim Rowley

If I set the expectation, train to the expectation, and have the team train it back, then I have to hold them accountable to it. That's the leadership coaching loop we talked about before. Because once the standard is clear, what I tolerate defines whether it's real.

If I tell someone, "This is the requirement for being a general manager, a vice president, or a senior vice president," and I've laid out those expectations in detail but then I allow something less, I've compromised. I can't preach excellence and then look the other way when someone misses the mark. The moment I do, my credibility takes a hit. My word doesn't mean what I said it did.

That's where a lot of leaders slip. They start making exceptions. They bend the rules for a favorite employee. They justify poor behavior because "that person produces." But every one of those exceptions chips away at integrity. You've been compromised as a leader.

You have to maintain these standards even when you're leading friends or people who were once your peers. That's one of the hardest transitions any leader will make. It takes me back to my time in the Marine Corps. We were all privates together, then one of us became a private first class, then a lance corporal, then a corporal, and so on. You keep getting elevated, but you're still in the same circle of people. Suddenly, you're leading those who once stood shoulder to shoulder with you.

That's when leadership becomes personal. You have to ask yourself: *Am I exhibiting and mirroring the right behaviors? Am I setting the standard of excellence that justifies my promotion?* Because now, those same peers are watching to see if your character matches your title. Do they see conviction, or compromise? Do they see a leader who walks the talk, or someone who folds when things get uncomfortable? And that's why it's hard for most. If I set a standard but don't back it up with accountability, I look weak; so many just don't set the standard.

That's the great separator. *But I want people to like me.* I get it, we all want to be liked. But this is your job, not your social circle. The real challenge of leadership isn't just managing others; it's mastering yourself. You have to know enough about all parts of the business to lead confidently, go deep when the moment requires it, and have the strategic gumption to turn information into action. Moving from peer to supervisor to leader is an evolution of your mindset more than it is just a promotion. You have to rise to the responsibility or you'll crumble under its weight.

That's why we do so much training around dialogue and self-awareness, because this is where most people quit. Leadership isn't a moment; it's a grind. It's constant. You have to manage pressure; stay composed; be the example; and remain the source of inspiration, motivation, and facts, month after month, year after year, decade after decade. That's perseverance. That's the never-quit mentality.

Everyone wants success, but few are willing to do what it takes to earn it. As we mentioned earlier, everyone wants to eat, but not everyone wants to hunt. Leadership is the hunt. It's the conviction, determination, and wherewithal to align your actions with your goals, even when it's uncomfortable. Because growth *is* uncomfortable. You'll be elevated above your peers. You'll make sacrifices. You'll create friction by holding a higher standard. But that's what separates the good from the great.

At the end of the day, there's no secret formula. It's about personal conviction aligned with professional purpose. It's about the motivation to hold yourself to the highest standard and the strength to do it consistently, even when it's hard. It's knowing that being a demanding, driven leader isn't a flaw; it's a responsibility.

And yes, some people will say you're tough, or hard, or demanding. But I've never met anyone who looked back at a strong, inspiring leader and said, "That was the worst leader I ever had." The ones people remember negatively are the inconsistent ones, the leaders who preach standards but tolerate anything. The ones who compromise their word.

We want to work for leaders who challenge us, who expect excellence, who inspire and push and develop us, but who also show empathy and care along the way. That balance is what creates trust. And while it's tough in the moment, it's what defines great leadership in the long run.

It's one of those tough mirror moments. You can say you want to be inspiring, hit goals, and get promoted; but if you're tolerating behavior that doesn't align with those ambitions, you're standing in your own way. The standard you walk past is the standard you accept.

People don't follow what you preach. They follow what you permit. They follow what you model. They follow what you fight for when it's uncomfortable.

And that's the real test of leadership. Not when things are easy. Not when everyone agrees. But in the hard moments: the late arrival, the missed target, the negative attitude, the quiet disrespect. Those moments decide everything.

> When you choose consistency over comfort, your culture gets stronger.
> When you choose clarity over compromise, your people get better.
> When you choose courage over convenience, your team learns to trust you.

Because a leader who won't tolerate mediocrity gives people permission to rise. A leader who protects the standard protects the team. A leader who refuses to compromise inspires others to level up.

In the long run, people don't remember the speeches. They remember the example. They remember the accountability. They remember the leader who upheld the standard even when it cost them.

> So if you want a culture of excellence, stop preaching it.
> **Start enforcing it.**
> Start embodying it.
> Start protecting it with the same intensity you expect from your team.

At the end of the day, leadership isn't just about hitting numbers; it's about trust. When your team sees that your words and actions line up, they believe in you. They know you mean what you say. That consistency builds respect, and respect builds culture. You can't demand accountability from others if you don't model it yourself. Integrity isn't a talking point; it's a daily choice. The standard starts and ends with you. Imagine years down the road one of your team members takes time to contact you and thank you for being their example of what leadership is supposed to look like because you set the standard.

TOOL: THE CULTURE CONTRACT

Use these three questions as your daily filter:

1. *What am I tolerating right now that undermines my culture?*
2. *What behavior am I rewarding, intentionally or not?*
3. *What's one standard I can reassert today?*

What you tolerate today becomes your culture tomorrow.

EXERCISE: ZERO TOLERANCE WEEK

For the next fourteen days, pick one behavior you've been tolerating that hurts your culture.

1. Announce to your team that this behavior is no longer acceptable.
2. Enforce it consistently for fourteen days. No exceptions.
3. At the end of the two weeks, evaluate: How did the team respond? Did standards rise? Did respect increase?

Repeat this process with a new behavior each month. Over time, your culture will shift dramatically

CHAPTER 9 VERY IMPORTANT POINTS

- What you tolerate today becomes your culture tomorrow.
- Standards are enforced in the uncomfortable moments, not the easy ones.
- Accountability is clarity, and clarity is kindness.
- Stop protecting feelings if it means compromising excellence.
- The scoreboard never lies, and neither does your performance.

CRUNCH

Chapter 10

WORK-LIFE BALANCE VS. WORK-LIFE HARMONY

The simplest way to live the life you want is to decide what that is and say no to everything that isn't. Simple, not easy.

—Alex Hormozi

Work-life balance is a myth. People talk about it like it's some magic formula, equal parts career, family, hobbies, health, relaxation, all perfectly measured and balanced. The truth? That balance doesn't exist. Life doesn't fit into neat little compartments.

When I say work-life balance is nonsense, I don't mean family or health don't matter. They matter deeply. What I mean is this: Leaders don't succeed by dividing themselves evenly. They succeed by bringing work-life harmony into their lives, setting clear priorities, and bringing full energy to whatever matters most in that season.

Think about it. There are times when business will require more from you, like when you're opening a new club, turning around a struggling team, or navigating a crisis. During those times, work takes more of your energy. Then there are times when family needs you more: kids, health, aging parents. Balance isn't about splitting evenly. It's about being all-in where you are, when you need to be.

At the end of the day, it all comes down to your goals. What do you want to achieve? If your goal is to be an employee or to sit comfortably in middle management, then sure, work-life balance might make sense. But if your goal is to run a business, to lead at the highest level, then **work-life balance** is out the window. **It's a trade-off.**

That doesn't mean you can't have harmony in your life. I still took vacations with my kids. We still made time for extracurricular activities. But let's get real. This idea that you can have a perfect 50/50 split between work and personal life? That's a myth. There will always be sacrifices. And anyone who tells you otherwise is selling you a lie. Can you find harmony? Yes. Can you lean into your family time and take breaks when needed? Absolutely. But it all hinges on what you're willing to give to achieve what you want. Your goals will dictate that balance or lack of it.

My friend **Tony Jeary** (who helped publish this tool in your hands that I only dreamed of creating) always says that achieving success starts with **clarity, focus, and execution**. You have to define your own vision because if you don't know exactly what you want, it's going to be impossible to find any kind of balance, let alone harmony. Without a clear direction, you're always playing catch-up. You can't move forward if you're not aligned with your vision. It's about matching your daily actions with where you want to go; and once you do that, everything else falls into place.

The Marines didn't give me "balance." They gave me clarity. The mission came first, and you brought everything you had. That carried into my career. When I'm in the club, I'm all-in. When I'm with my family, I'm present. What I don't do is pretend I can slice life into perfect fractions.

Here's the trap: Leaders who chase "balance" often end up mediocre everywhere. They spread themselves thin, constantly apologizing to both sides, never going deep enough in either. Leaders who embrace harmony, on the other hand, live with more clarity and less guilt. It's fluid. They choose priorities and go hard.

Think about athletes or musicians: people who dedicate their lives to mastering their craft. The amount of time they invest in training, diet, nutrition, and travel is insane. If you're a golfer, a football player, or an F1 driver, you're constantly on the road. You're away from family and living out of a suitcase. Now, **is there balance in that lifestyle?** Not the kind of balance most people imagine. They'll tell you about the "off-season" where they have more time for themselves or their family but that's not the balance we're talking about. The reality is, those athletes are 100 percent committed to their craft, and everything else revolves around it. Even in the off season, they're training and honing their skills. They're having to be nutritionally sound, they're having to exercise, they're having to keep up with all the expectations for the next season. As the saying goes, "The grind don't stop."

Take overachievers in other fields, like doctors. How do you expect balance during med school, residency, or when you're on call, working 36-hour shifts? **There's no perfect balance in those early years**. It's all about the long-term goal. You define your aspirations, and then you figure out how to make it work. Yes, you take care of yourself and your family, but **balance** in the traditional sense? It doesn't always exist in the way people think.

When I think about my own family, it was never about the *quantity* of time, it was about the *quality*. I traveled constantly, I was on planes all the time; but when I was home, I made sure I was fully present. I coached my kids, I stayed involved, and I made those moments count. **It's not about trying to be everywhere; it's about making sure you're fully where you are.**

The sooner you let go of the myth of balance and embrace the harmony, the better leader you'll become.

Harmony beats illusion every time.

We recently had our franchise owners' conference in Jackson Hole, Wyoming. At the same time, my son was getting married. Now, the dates didn't overlap, but the wedding was on a Saturday, and the conference started Sunday. I would've had to fly straight from the wedding to the conference. But here's the thing, I still had family in town. My son and his new wife, my other kids, and distant relatives were all there, celebrating.

I made the decision not to go to the owners' summit. And that was the first time in my career that I consciously put family over work. Normally, I would've hopped on a plane Sunday, flown from Hawaii to Wyoming, and been there like I always was. But I felt like my team had it. **They were capable, and I trusted them to manage the event without me.**

And guess what? The event in Wyoming was a success. Sure, my absence was felt, but it didn't derail the conference or affect the value that everyone got from it. That's what work-life harmony looks like. Sometimes, it's about making that hard call to be present for your family when it matters most and trusting your team to carry the load. It worked out, and in the end, we all benefited from it.

Now let me take you back to the early days of building Crunch. This time, I had to do the opposite. I had to prioritize work over family to make it all work. At the time, I was living in California, but the office was based in New York. So I was flying to New York a lot, Monday through Friday. I always tried to get home by Friday if I could, but there were times when that just wasn't possible.

Here's where the harmony comes in. I coached my kids' sports teams; and when I was in the US, I made it a priority to be home on Fridays to attend their games, to participate as a coach, and be involved in their lives. But for a lot of the week, I was in New York, building strategy, assembling the team, hiring people, and doing the operational work to build the company.

In my mind, it was always about the bigger picture. These were the sacrifices I had to make in order to build something that would provide my family with opportunities: great vacations, private schooling, and the ability to put all three of my kids through college without their having to worry about tuition. These were the hard decisions I made early on, so they wouldn't have a financial burden down the road.

The question I always wrestled with was, **"Am I doing right by them as a father by giving them these opportunities, or am I doing wrong by being away from them so much to achieve it?"** Those are the tough decisions I had to make, and I don't regret them. It was part of building the future I wanted for my family; and sometimes, that meant making the tough call to put in the hours and days away to create the legacy I wanted to leave. In all honesty, I've also had the greatest gift: a spouse at home who created an environment that made this work.

TOOL: THE INTEGRATION MAP

Instead of asking, *"How do I balance everything?"* ask: *What matters most right now, and how do I show up fully?*

1. **Identify the Season** — Work surge? Family focus? Personal growth?
2. **Clarify Priorities** — Choose your top 3 (not 10).
3. **Set Boundaries** — Define when and where you'll be fully engaged.
4. **Communicate Clearly** — Let your team and family know what to expect.
5. **Review Often** — Adjust as seasons shift.

EXERCISE: BROWN BAG DRILL

1. Before your next shift, meeting, or training session, write down everything on your mind: personal stress, unfinished tasks, worries.
2. Fold the paper, put it in a bag or drawer.
3. Say out loud: *"I'll pick this up later. Right now, my team gets my best."*
4. Walk into the room focused, present, and all-in.

Repeat daily for a week. Notice how much more energy and clarity you bring when you check the bag at the door.

"Balance is a mirage. What matters is clarity: knowing when to go all-in on the mission and when to go all-in at home."

– Jim Rowley

CHAPTER 10 VERY IMPORTANT POINTS

- Balance is a myth; clarity and intentional focus create real harmony.
- Seasons shift, so should your priorities; be all-in where it matters most.
- Harmony means trade-offs, not guilt; success requires conscious sacrifices.

- Presence beats perfection; quality of engagement outweighs quantity.
- Leave the baggage at the door; your team needs your leadership, not your stress.

Chapter 11

EVERYONE IS LEVERAGED

"Success isn't just about what you do personally. It's about who you develop, how you multiply yourself, and the leaders you leave behind."

– Jim Rowley

Leadership is leverage. It's the ability to multiply your impact through people, systems, and influence. The best leaders understand this early. The worst leaders drown under tasks they should have delegated years ago.

When I say *everyone is leveraged*, I mean this: You're either leveraging your people, time, and influence to expand your capacity, or the business is leveraging **you**: pulling you into every crisis, every decision, every fire. There is no middle ground.

I've watched leaders burn out because they refused to let go. They clung to responsibilities out of fear or ego. They thought *No one can do it as well as I can.* That's not leadership; that's insecurity. True leadership is building people who can carry the mission with you and eventually without you.

At Crunch, that's why we're always developing the bench. Not because it's a nice idea, but because it's a requirement. If someone leaves and there's no one ready to step in, that isn't a staffing problem; that's a leadership problem. Strong organizations don't scramble; they transition.

While I'm aligning and motivating current leaders, I'm also investing in the next layer: those who show hunger, humility, and potential. My time is leveraged between both levels. That's intentional. It's how continuity, culture, and capacity scale.

But here's the part people forget: **People often feel ready before the business is.** Part of leadership is keeping them encouraged, challenged, and growing, even during the waiting seasons. Yes, you may lose someone occasionally. That's reality. But waiting doesn't mean they're being ignored; it means you're preparing them wisely.

The Marines ingrained this in me. You train your replacement from day one. If you go down, the mission doesn't. That mindset shaped my entire career. If you're not building people who can step up, you're not leading; you're just occupying a title.

Leadership isn't static. It's a continual cycle of observing, mentoring, delegating, and empowering. Promotion isn't the finish line; it's the starting line for developing others.

I've seen franchisees build empires because they built depth: assistant managers ready to be GMs, trainers prepared for leadership, front-line staff developing operational understanding. And I've seen the opposite: owners who micromanaged every detail, exhausted themselves and their teams, and watched performance collapse the moment they stepped away.

Leverage is happening whether you acknowledge it or not. Your **money** is leveraged when it works without you. Your **time** is leveraged when you coach instead of doing. Your **influence** is leveraged when leaders you've developed produce results in markets you've never stepped foot in.

The question is: **Are you leveraging your world or is your world leveraging you?**

Now, a key truth: Strong leaders don't cling to top performers. They create an environment where top performers grow. It's not about repeating past examples of talent development; it's about understanding the deeper principle: **A leader's capacity is measured by how many people rise because of them.** You don't fear losing great people. You expect it. You plan for it. You take pride in it. Because every time someone you trained steps into a bigger role, your influence scales again. That's leverage.

One of the proudest measures of success for me has been watching people who worked with me rise into leadership roles across the industry. Some became GMs. Some became franchise owners. Some went on to run different companies. At first, it stung to lose great people. But I realized that's the mark of true leadership: when the leaders you develop go on to build their own dynasties. At Crunch, I've encouraged franchisees to adopt the same mindset. Don't cling to talent because you're afraid of losing them. Build them, promote them, and let them rise.

When your system exports leaders, your influence multiplies far beyond your own four walls.

TOOL: THE LEVERAGE LADDER

1. **Do It Yourself** — You carry the weight. No leverage.
2. **Delegate Tasks** — You hand off work, but keep ownership.
3. **Develop People** — You build leaders who can own outcomes.
4. **Export Talent** — You send those leaders into bigger roles and new markets.
5. **Multiply Influence** — Your systems, culture, and people expand results without your direct involvement.

Climbing this ladder is the essence of leadership growth.

EXERCISE: LEVERAGE AUDIT

1. Write down your top ten weekly tasks.
2. Circle which ones could be delegated or taught to someone else.
3. Identify one person you could develop to take over a key responsibility.
4. Build a thirty-day plan to train and empower them.

"If you're not exporting leaders, you're not leading. You're hoarding."
— *Jim Rowley*

CHAPTER 11 VERY IMPORTANT POINTS

- Success scales only when leaders multiply themselves through others.
- Your influence is measured by how many people can perform without you in the room.
- Developing leaders is not optional; it is the job.
- Holding onto tasks out of fear chokes growth and creates bottlenecks.
- Legacy is built through people, not personal output.

Part IV

CHARACTER, AUTHENTICITY, AND ENDURANCE

Sustainable leadership depends on integrity, humility, and humanity; staying authentic, owning mistakes, and remembering that influence is earned through consistency, not titles.

Chapter 12

LEADERSHIP IS A RESPONSIBILITY, NOT A TITLE

"Leadership isn't given. It's earned every day, in every decision. A title doesn't make you a leader. Responsibility does."

– Jim Rowley

Too many people chase titles. They think if they become a general manager, a regional, a VP, or even a CEO, then, finally, they'll be a leader. But leadership has nothing to do with the letters on your business card. Leadership is about responsibility: taking ownership for outcomes, for people, and for culture.

In the Marines, few people cared about titles. What mattered was whether you did your job, took care of your team, and executed the mission. If you failed in those responsibilities, your rank meant nothing. That lesson shaped everything I've done in business.

At Crunch, I've seen this play out again and again. You may remember my story about the front-desk associate with zero formal authority who stepped up, took responsibility for the member experience, and became a leader in the eyes of the entire team. Other times, we've had managers with a title but no accountability who would erode trust and generally drag the culture down. Leadership isn't about where you sit on the org chart. It's about whether you accept responsibility when it matters.

Here's the truth: **Titles give you authority. Responsibility gives you influence.** Authority fades the moment people stop respecting it. Influence grows when people trust you. You can demand compliance with a title, but you only inspire commitment through responsibility.

Responsibility also means owning the bad along with the good. When the team misses a goal, leaders take the hit. When the team wins, leaders give the credit away. Weak leaders flip that script. They blame when it's bad and brag when it's good. But people see through it. True leaders carry the weight of the mission, no matter what.

Every franchisee, every GM, every team leader in this organization should remember: The privilege of leadership comes with the price of responsibility. You don't get to clock out on culture. You don't get to ignore accountability. You don't get to say, "That's not my problem." If you wear the mantle of leader, everything is your problem.

Everyone says they want to lead. They want the title and the paycheck. But not everyone wants the responsibility that comes with it. That's the real separator between average leaders and great ones. Leadership isn't about the position; it's about the relationships you build, the consistency you show, and the investment you make in your people. That's where credibility is earned and that's what sustains real leadership.

Don't chase the title. Embrace the responsibility.

LEADERSHIP INVERTED: THE SERVANT MODEL

Early in your leadership journey, there's a trap that's easy to fall into, especially right after a promotion. You start to believe the team is there to serve you. You earned your stripes, and now it's their job to report, execute, and salute.

But that mindset kills influence.

Let me flip it for you: **The team doesn't serve you. You serve the team.**

The more you invest in their development, the more you ask how you can help, the more you pour into their growth and confidence, the more they'll pour into the business. It's not about lowering standards; it's about lifting people to meet them.

That's the inverted pyramid.

Instead of standing on top barking orders, great leaders go underneath and lift. They ask:

- "How can I help you sell more?"
- "Where are you stuck?"

- "What's your personal goal this month?"
- "Let me hear your pitch. Let's refine it together."

Some might call that soft. It's not. It's strength in action.

And make no mistake: Servant leadership is demanding. But it demands more of yourself before it demands anything from others.

A servant leader doesn't just want results; they want their team to own the results. They build people, not just performance charts.

I've seen both types of leaders:

- The insecure one who says, "I'm the boss. Show me your numbers."
- And the servant leader who says, "I'm here to help you win. Let's get after it, together."

Which one would you follow?

Look at any corporate event you attend. Do you think it's for the owner? No. It's for you. All the time, travel, and energy are being done to make you better. That's what servant leadership looks like behind the curtain.

So here's the challenge: **Invert your mindset. Serve first. Grow your people. Earn their trust.**

That's leadership that lasts.

CONNECTION MATTERS

Great culture defines, sustains, and grows an organization. It's the heartbeat of everything we do. As leaders, our job is to create and protect that culture to make sure our people feel connected to something bigger than themselves.

For us, that means shared values, a shared vision, and shared accountability. It means surrounding ourselves with great talent, modeling the right behaviors, and uniting around a clear purpose. When we get that right, hierarchy fades. Titles matter less because everyone is rowing in the same direction.

That's when the magic happens: when leadership becomes a culture, not a position.

My role as a leader is to build that culture to be a culture of winning, excellence, and the relentless pursuit of greatness. And it starts with me. I hold myself accountable. I reflect. I communicate. I plan. I coach. I grow alongside my team.

Because when people feel emotionally connected, when they know their leader is all in with them, motivation turns into momentum, and momentum turns into results.

Connection matters. Too many leaders make it all about their goals, their numbers, their grind. But real leadership is about knowing your people, professionally *and* personally. If you can't name what your members are doing personally, you're missing half the picture.

> Your job isn't just to lead. It's to know.
> Know what drives them.
> Know their pressure points.
> Know where they shine.
> Know where they struggle.

The stronger the connection, the stronger the commitment. And commitment drives results.

One of the most underrated habits of great leadership is the monthly one-on-one. I'm not talking about formal evaluations. I mean intentional, consistent check-ins where you actually know your people.

Five to thirty minutes. Personal first. Business second. Always real.

This rhythm builds trust, surfaces problems early, and creates genuine ownership. It's not optional. It's part of the job. Leadership isn't just directing; it's connecting. If your team doesn't feel seen, they won't follow you when it gets hard. If they do, they'll go through walls for you.

Great leaders know their people.

TOOL: THE RESPONSIBILITY EQUATION

Responsibility = Ownership + Accountability + Service

- **Ownership** — The willingness to say, *This is mine to solve.*
- **Accountability** — The desire to measure results and face reality.
- **Service** — The commitment to put the team and mission above yourself.

Titles expire. **Responsibility endures.**

TOOL: OPERATING SYSTEM FOR MANAGERS

1. Have a plan
2. Communicate effectively
3. Build culture

4. Lead by example
5. Coach constantly
6. Be present

Details matter.

EXERCISE

1. **Schedule It**
   - A fifteen-to-thirty-minute monthly one-on-one with each team member.
   - Make it recurring. Non-negotiable.
2. **Prep for It**
   - Review last month's notes and numbers.
   - Think about their *personal* and professional goals.
3. **Run It Like This**
   - **Start Personal:** "How are you doing?" "What's new outside the club?"
   - **Get Tactical:** "Where are you winning?" "What's blocking you?"
   - **Coach Up:** Feedback, challenge, clarity.
   - **End With Support:** "What do you need from me?"
4. **Track It**
   - Take a note.
   - Follow up next month.

Bonus Tip: If you don't know their spouse/partner's name, their kids' names, their hobbies, or what lights them up, you have homework to do.

EXERCISE: RESPONSIBILITY REFLECTION

1. List three areas where you currently carry responsibility.
2. Ask: *Am I owning these fully, or am I relying on my title to cover me?*
3. Identify one area where you've been avoiding responsibility.
4. Take one action this week to step up and own it, without waiting for recognition.

Leadership isn't about the stripes on your sleeve or the letters after your name. **It's about what you carry when it counts.**

"Titles sit on paper.
Responsibility lives in action."
– Unknown

CHAPTER 12 VERY IMPORTANT POINTS

- Titles sit on paper; responsibility lives in action.
- Real leaders lean in before recognition and stay accountable after mistakes.

- Presence, discipline, and example outrank authority every time.
- Respect is earned through consistency, not hierarchy.
- Leadership begins the moment you choose to own the outcome.
- Get to know your team.

CRUNCH

Chapter 13

CHARACTER MATTERS

"You live in a fishbowl as a leader.
Every move you make is watched.
Every inconsistency gets magnified."
—Jim Rowley

Leadership isn't about what you carry. It's about what you multiply.

At the end of the day, leadership is revealed when no one is clapping, when no metrics are flashing green, and when no one is standing behind you pushing you forward. It's revealed in the moments when you do the right thing simply because it *is* the right thing. In this business, and in life, you don't rise to the level of your goals; you fall to the level of your character.

Titles expire. Trends change. Strategies evolve. But character endures. It's the one competitive advantage no one can steal, no downturn can erase, and no shortcut can replace. Your team will remember how you made decisions when the pressure was on, how you treated people when no one was looking, and how you showed up when things were hard.

Your leadership legacy won't be written in numbers. It'll be written in the people who chose to follow you. And they will only follow a leader whose character they trust. So guard it. Sharpen it. Live it daily.

NON-NEGOTIABLE DAILY ACTIONS OF A LEADER

When I think about the things that separate the professionals from the pretenders, it always starts with example. In our business, that means showing up on time, in uniform, name tag on, shirt tucked in, ready to go. You can't ask for standards you don't live yourself. Leadership begins with presence. If I expect my team to look sharp and be ready, I have to model that from the moment I walk through the door.

The next non-negotiable is coming in mission-specific. Every day has to start with clarity. What's the plan? What's the goal? What's the objective? You can't just "show up and see what happens." You have to meet with your team, assess the setup for the day, and decide whether you're positioned for success or for struggle. And if the setup isn't right, you adjust it before the day gets away from you. That's how you build consistency in performance.

Third, in our business, you do a club walk. And that starts before you ever step inside. From the moment you get out of the car, you're looking at the business through your member's eyes. Is the parking lot clean? Are the garbage cans empty? Is the sidewalk clear, the glass spotless? When you step inside, is the front desk decluttered? Is the energy professional and welcoming? Then you walk the entire club with that same critical eye: the locker rooms, the music, the temperature, the smell, the supplies. Everything speaks. You can't lead from your desk if you haven't taken the pulse of your business.

Fourth, you plan your own day. Who are you meeting with? Who do you need to coach, develop, or recognize today? What are your own personal goals for the day? Leadership isn't about staying busy; it's about staying intentional. You have to hold yourself to the same expectations you set for your team.

Next, you check your energy. As Jack Welch indicated in his 4 E's, leaders have to have energy, and they have to energize others. That means managing your mindset before you walk in. If you're not in a positive frame of mind, you fix it before you hit the floor. Leadership demands presence, focus, and energy.

And finally, you set the expectations and demonstrate the behaviors you want your team to emulate. For example:

- Make the first sale of the day.
- Talk to your members.
- Answer the phone.
- Take the angry complaint yourself.

Those are the four daily actions that set the tone for everything else. They're not just habits of performance; they're reflections of character. You don't just lead by what you achieve. You lead by who you are. And who you are is the one thing that always shows.

I often use Sunday at 4pm, a time for quiet reflection of what I want to accomplish in the week ahead, and I write my plan.

At the end of the day, leadership isn't about projecting strength, it's about building it in others. And you can't do that if you're hiding behind armor. People don't need a flawless commander; they need a real human being who leads with honesty, humor, humility, and ownership.

You can be strong and human. You can be demanding and compassionate. You can hold the line and still admit when you've crossed it. That blend is what makes leadership sustainable, not brittle. Because when your team sees you as human, they don't just follow your title. They follow your example.

And here's the truth you can't escape: Your team will give you the same level of humanity you give them. If you're honest, they'll be honest. If you're approachable, they'll come forward early instead of waiting until a small issue explodes. If you model vulnerability, they'll trust you enough to try, to stretch, to learn.

Being human isn't the opposite of being a leader. Being human is what makes leadership work.

Because at the end of your career, no one will remember the flawless days. They'll remember the real ones; the moments you owned your mistakes, lifted someone up, or showed the courage to say, "I don't have it all figured out; but I'm here, and I'm with you."

That's humanity.
That's leadership.
And that's what people follow.

TOOL: THE CHARACTER COMPASS

Check yourself against these four directions:

1. **North: Integrity** — Do you keep promises and honor commitments?
2. **East: Humility** — Do you listen, learn, and give credit?
3. **South: Consistency** — Do you show up the same way, day after day?
4. **West: Courage** — Do you make the hard calls even when they're unpopular?

If your compass points are aligned, your leadership will stay true.

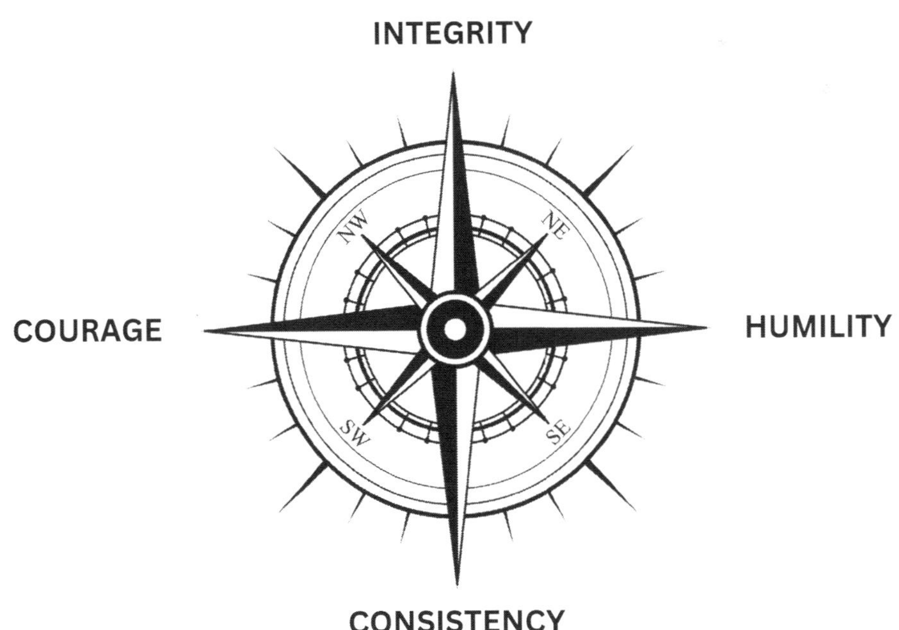

EXERCISE: THE MIRROR TEST

Tonight, look in the mirror and ask yourself:

1. *Did I model the behaviors I expect from my team today?*
2. *Did I give credit where it was due?*
3. *Did I own my mistakes without excuses?*
4. *Did I make at least one hard decision instead of avoiding it?*

If the answer is "no" to any, write down how you'll correct it tomorrow. Repeat this exercise for 30 days. Character is built through daily discipline.

> "If you demand standards from others but don't keep them yourself, you're not a leader. You're a hypocrite."
>
> *– Jim Rowley*

CHAPTER 13 VERY IMPORTANT POINTS

- *Titles, strategies, and results may change, but character is what people remember and trust.*
- *Leaders must model the standards they expect.*
- *Character is built through repeated actions.*
- *Strong leaders are honest, humble, approachable, and willing to own mistakes. People follow leaders who are real, not flawless.*

Chapter 14

IT'S OKAY TO BE HUMAN

"I'm a Marine, I'm a CEO, but I'm also a husband, a father, a guy who makes mistakes. Being human isn't weakness; it's what makes leadership real."

– Jim Rowley

There's a dangerous myth in leadership: that you have to be invincible. Leaders convince themselves they can never show weakness, never admit mistakes, never let people see behind the armor. But here's the truth: Pretending to be perfect doesn't make people respect you more. It makes them trust you less.

Being human doesn't mean being sloppy. It doesn't mean lowering standards. It means showing your team that you're real. It means admitting when you're wrong, asking for help when you need it, and showing that leadership is a journey, not a destination.

The Marines trained me to be tough, but they also trained me to rely on my brothers. No Marine fights alone. We leaned on each other, admitted when we were at our limits, and built strength together. That same principle works in business. Leaders who isolate themselves, who try to carry everything alone, eventually break. Leaders who show humanity build loyalty, connection, and resilience.

I've sat in franchisee meetings where someone broke down over personal struggles. Instead of judging them, the room leaned in. That vulnerability built bonds stronger than any quarterly report could. I've admitted mistakes to my own teams and watched their respect for me grow, not shrink. People don't expect perfection from leaders. They expect honesty.

Being human also means giving yourself grace. This business is demanding; it requires long hours, constant pressure, and the weight of leading teams and serving members. If you beat yourself up for every misstep, you'll burn out. Instead, acknowledge your humanity, learn from it, and move forward.

At Crunch, we work hard, but we also laugh hard. Humor is part of our culture because it keeps us grounded. If we can't be human together, we'll break under the weight of always trying to be superhuman.

Leadership is serious. But leaders don't have to act like robots. Humanity is what makes people want to follow you, not just your rank, but your realness.

Remember, though, a leader's job is to practice honest signaling without slipping into self-indulgence. It's easy to assume that when something's not working, whether it's motivation, execution, or behavior, it's the team that's the problem. But the best leaders flip that. They pause, reflect, and ask: *"What role am I playing in this outcome?"* That's not weakness; that's leadership. You have to be honest with yourself, even when it's a hard pill to swallow.

Early in my career, I missed an important call with a franchise partner because of a travel delay. I could have blamed the airline, the schedule, or the chaos of the road. Instead, I owned it. I called the partner directly, apologized sincerely, and admitted I had overcommitted my time. You know what happened? They respected me more. They saw I was human, not a machine. That moment built more trust than any polished speech ever could.

Sometimes, the issue isn't the employee; it's the way we're leading them. Maybe your communication style isn't landing. Maybe your approach isn't connecting. That's where self-regulation and adaptability matter. Early in my journey, I dove deep into **neuro-linguistic programming**. It taught me something simple but powerful: *not everyone learns the same way.* If you're really going to invest in your team and learn about them as individuals, you need to understand how they learn best.

- Do they need to see it before they learn it?
- Do they learn best by hearing it and seeing it?
- Do they need to do it alongside a coach to internalize it?

The military didn't care about that. They used repetition as the learning tool. You were told once, one way, and it was sink or swim. That might work in combat, but in business, you're building people, not breaking them.

Great leaders meet people where they are. That means investing time to understand how each team member learns, processes feedback, and responds to coaching. You can't be so rigid that it's "my way or the highway." If that's your mindset, don't be surprised when you're constantly churning through team members. That's not leadership—that's just cycling failure.

Take the time to reflect on your **coaching style, communication method, and how you enforce accountability.** Are they helping or hurting? And here's the bigger truth: *You're always being watched.* We all live in a goldfish bowl. If you're asking your team to meet high standards but you're not living by them yourself, your credibility's shot. Accountability starts with you.

TOOL: THE HUMANITY CHECK

Ask yourself these questions weekly:

1. **Am I approachable?** Do people feel safe bringing me problems?
2. **Am I honest?** Do I admit when I don't know or when I'm wrong?
3. **Am I balanced?** Do I allow humor, humility, and grace in my leadership?
4. **Am I connected?** Do I know something about my people beyond their job description?

If you can't say yes to each of these questions, you're leading from a pedestal, not from the trenches.

EXERCISE: THE VULNERABILITY SHARE

At your next team meeting, take five minutes to share one mistake you've made recently, what you learned, and how you corrected it.

1. Keep it short and honest.
2. Invite your team to share their own lessons learned.
3. Celebrate the growth, not just the outcome.

Do this once a month. You'll be amazed how much loyalty and connection grow when people see that it's okay to be human.

EXERCISE: COMMUNICATION IS KEY

Write your "three true things" you will share with your team this quarter.

1. ______________________________
2. ______________________________
3. ______________________________

"Perfection is fake. Humanity is real.
And people follow what's real."

—Jim Rowley

CHAPTER 14 VERY IMPORTANT POINTS

- Being human and real builds far more trust than pretending to be invincible.
- Admitting mistakes, asking for help, and owning your role in outcomes is not weakness; it is leadership.
- Vulnerability, humor, and grace keep you and your team grounded, connected, and resilient.
- Great leaders adapt their communication and coaching to how each person learns best.
- You are always on stage as a leader, so your behavior must consistently match the standards you expect from others.

Part V

CASCADING TRAINING MODULES

Cascading training is how culture scales. When leaders train with intention, behaviors spread: down, across, and throughout the entire organizational network. The following modules are designed to be simple, repeatable, and high-impact. Each one reinforces the standards, mindset, and grit required to build high-performing teams.

1. MEDIOCRITY: THE STANDARD DROP MODEL

Concept:

Mediocrity isn't neutral. It's contagious. When leaders tolerate "good enough," performance declines everywhere.

Model: The Standard Drop

1. **Leader Tolerates** — One person slips.
2. **Team Copies** — Others see the slip is allowed.
3. **Culture Shifts** — Average becomes acceptable.
4. **Results Decline** — Goals missed, morale drops.

Exercise:

- Write down one area where you've been tolerating mediocrity (lateness, messy sales floor, sloppy reporting).
    - ____
      ____
      ____
- Set a new standard this week: announce it clearly and enforce it consistently.
- Track the ripple effect for 30 days.

2. COMPETITION IS GOOD: THE RIVALRY MODEL

Concept:

Competition sharpens performance. Without it, teams go stale.

Model: The Healthy Rivalry Loop

1. **Set the Scoreboard** — Publish results for everyone to see.
2. **Create Rivalries** — Pair teams, clubs, or individuals head-to-head.
3. **Celebrate Winners** — Public recognition fuels motivation.
4. **Reset the Game** — Start the next round to keep momentum.

Exercise:

- Pick one key metric (PT sessions, sales, renewals).
  - ____
    ____
    ____
- Run a two-week competition between two teams or clubs.
- Post daily results on a public scoreboard.
- Celebrate the winner and debrief lessons learned.

3. GRIT: THE 3-R RULE

Concept:
Grit is resilience plus persistence: what keeps teams in the fight when things get hard.

Model: The 3-R Rule

- **Resist:** Don't quit when the pressure hits.
- **Recover:** Bounce back quickly from setbacks.
- **Repeat:** Keep showing up consistently.

Exercise:

- Have each team member identify one current obstacle.
  - ____
    ____
  - ____
    ____
  - ____
    ____
  - ____
    ____
  - ____
    ____
- Ask them to apply the 3-R Rule: How will they resist, recover, and repeat?
- Share answers in a team huddle.

4. MINDSET: THE SHIFT FRAMEWORK

Concept:

Outcomes follow mindset. The right mental state can be trained and taught.

Model: The SHIFT Framework

- **See It:** Identify your current mindset (negative, neutral, or positive).
- **Hold It:** Take ownership: no hiding, no blaming.
- **Interrupt It:** Use a reset technique (breathing, movement, humor).
- **Flip It:** Reframe the situation as an opportunity.
- **Train It:** Practice daily until it becomes habit.

Exercise:

- During your next team meeting, ask: "What's one negative thought we can flip right now?"
- Walk through SHIFT together.
- Post the flipped version where everyone can see it.

5. FITFO: THE FIGURE-IT-THE-F*-OUT DRILL

Concept:

Leaders solve problems. FITFO builds self-reliance, creativity, and confidence.

Model: The FITFO Decision Tree

1. **Face It:** Identify the roadblock clearly.
2. **Invent It:** Brainstorm three possible solutions.
3. **Test It:** Choose one and act.
4. **Fix It:** Adjust if it doesn't work.
5. **Own It:** Take responsibility for the result.

Exercise:

- The next time a team member brings you a problem, *don't give them the answer.*
- Ask them to propose three solutions.
- Walk them through the FITFO Tree.
- Over time, train them to bring solutions first and problems second.

CRUNCH

CONCLUSION

If you've made it this far, you understand something most people never will: Leadership isn't a title you chase, a role you inherit, or a moment you arrive at. It's a daily decision. A responsibility. Every chapter in this book has been building to one truth; the greatest leaders are forged in the small moments, the unseen reps, the uncomfortable conversations, the standards you refuse to lower, and the people you choose to lift along the way.

You've learned that culture doesn't happen by accident. Excellence doesn't happen by chance. Winning doesn't happen because you're lucky. It happens because leaders like you decide that mediocrity has no home in your organization. It happens because you embrace competition, develop grit, choose mindset over circumstance, and take responsibility, whether the spotlight is on you or not.

What the chapters in this book should make clear is this: **Leadership is not about becoming more important. It's about becoming more useful.**

It's about doing the work when no one is watching and preparing others to win when everyone is.

But here's the truth I need you to sit with: **Everything up to now has only been preparation.**

The real transformation happens in what comes next: in how you operationalize these ideas, how you cascade them through your teams, and how you build leaders who build leaders who build leaders. Because the ultimate test of leadership is not what you can personally achieve; it's what continues to grow long after you're gone.

As you do that work, remember this: Not everything you try is going to land perfectly. You will roll out ideas that don't get traction, make hires that aren't the right fit, launch initiatives that fall short. That doesn't mean the principles in this book are broken. It means you're in the arena. When that happens, go back to the fundamentals, stay true to the standards you've set, and keep moving forward. The leaders who win over time aren't the ones who never fail; they're the ones who keep applying the right principles even after they do.

So take a breath. Reflect on how far you've come in these pages.

You're not at the end.

You're at the beginning of who you're about to become.

Appendix

TOOLS, EXERCISES, AND VIPS

Chapter 1

TOOL: THE LEADERSHIP SELF-CHECK

Write down one leadership challenge you currently face. Then ask:

- ***Where am I waiting instead of leading?***
- ***What part of this situation do I own?***
- ***What action can I take within the next 24 hours?***

Stop waiting. Start leading.

TOOL: THE OWNERSHIP LADDER

Step 1: Excuses—*It's not my fault.*

Step 2: Blame—*If only corporate/my boss/the market did X.*

Step 3: Acknowledgment—*I had a role in this outcome.*

Step 4: Responsibility—*It's on me to fix this.*

Step 5: Ownership—*The result is mine to deliver. Period.*

Leaders who climb this ladder stop asking, "Who will help me?" and start saying, "What can I do right now?"

Credited to Bruce Gordon.

EXERCISE: OWNERSHIP AUDIT

List the top three problems in your business right now. Next to each:

- Circle "Waiting" if you expect someone else to solve it.

- Circle "Owning" if you're actively leading the fix.

Shift one "Waiting" to "Owning" this week and build a real plan to close the gap.

CHAPTER 1 VERY IMPORTANT POINTS

- Leadership starts the moment you accept that no one is coming to save you.
- Excuses kill execution; ownership accelerates results.
- Data must drive direction or you're flying blind.
- Weak teams wait. Strong teams prepare, analyze, and act.
- Leadership is responsibility, not rescue.

Chapter 2

TOOL: THE CULTURE FILTER

Before you bring someone onto your team, run them through this:

- **Drama:** Do they shut it down or stir it up?
- **Energy:** Do they raise the room or drain it?
- **Humility:** Do they say "we" more than "me"?
- **Resilience:** Do they face challenges or fold?
- **Respect:** Do they treat people well—members, teammates, leaders?

If they fail even one, they fail the filter.

EXERCISE: CULTURE STANDARDS AUDIT

1. List the last three times your team missed a goal.

____

____

____

2. Identify whether each miss was caused by lack of skill or lack of standards.
3. If it was standards, ask: *What did I tolerate?*
4. Write down three non-negotiable behaviors you will no longer allow.

____

____

____

5. Share them in your next team meeting and uphold them.

CHAPTER 2 VERY IMPORTANT POINTS

- Culture is built on standards, not slogans.
- The moment you tolerate excuses, you forfeit excellence.
- High standards attract high performers; low standards invite drama.
- Discipline beats talent when talent gets soft.
- Comfort is the enemy; choose the hard that pays off.

Chapter 3

TOOL: THE FIVE DNA MARKERS

1. **Humility** — Puts the team above self
2. **Perseverance** — Shows up even when it's difficult
3. **Loyalty** — Stays true in both good times and bad
4. **Coachability** — Seeks feedback and acts on it
5. **Finish Energy** — Completes what they start

When evaluating candidates or talent, score them on these five. Anyone can fake it for a day but DNA reveals itself over time.

EXERCISE: DNA INTERVIEW

Next time you're hiring or even evaluating your current team, try this:

1. Ask each person to tell a story about a time they failed. Watch how they describe it. Do they blame others, or do they own it?
2. Ask them who influenced them most growing up. Look for gratitude, humility, and respect.
3. Ask about a time they finished something difficult when no one was watching.

The answers will reveal their DNA faster than any résumé ever will.

EXERCISE

Write down the top 10 impactful moments in your life that you'd be comfortable sharing with others:

1. ____
2. ____
3. ____
4. ____
5. ____
6. ____
7. ____
8. ____
9. ____
10. ____

CHAPTER 3 VERY IMPORTANT POINTS

- DNA matters more than résumés; character outperforms credentials.
- Humility, loyalty, perseverance, and finish energy predict long-term success.
- Curiosity, preparation, and self-awareness reveal real leadership potential.
- Your story is fuel, not an anchor. Lead from what shaped you.
- Leaders win by betting on people whose habits match the mission.

Chapter 4

TOOL: THE FOUR ASSESSMENTS

Before acting on your gut, run yourself through these quick checks:

1. **Self-Awareness** — *How do I feel right now? Am I grounded or reactive?*
2. **Self-Regulation** — *What can I do to shift my mindset or reset my state?*
3. **Situational Awareness** — *How are others feeling? What's the emotional temperature of the room?*
4. **Situational Regulation** — *What can I influence right now to move things forward?*

These checks sharpen your instincts and keep your decisions aligned.

EXERCISE: THE GUT DRILL

This week, pick three decisions you've been delaying: big or small.

1. Limit yourself to five minutes of review for each.
   a. ______________________________
   b. ______________________________
   c. ______________________________
2. Run through the four assessments quickly for each.
3. Make the call.
4. Record the result and reflect: Was your gut right? If not, what can you learn to refine it?

CHAPTER 4 VERY IMPORTANT POINTS

- Perfect information never arrives; decisive leaders move anyway.
- Gut instinct is earned through discipline, reps, and self-awareness.
- Preparation sharpens intuition; hesitation dulls it.
- Asking the right questions is often more powerful than having the right answers.
- Confidence comes from clarity and presence, not bravado.

Chapter 5

TOOL: THE T-MODEL LEADER

Picture the letter T.

- The **vertical stroke** is your deep area of expertise: the thing you know inside and out.
- The **horizontal stroke** is your breadth: the "little about a lot" knowledge that connects everything else.

Strong leaders are T-shaped. They go deep where they must, but they also go wide enough to understand, connect, and challenge across disciplines.

To be successful and highly effective in your teamwork responsibilities, you will need to know about and exercise both leadership and management behaviors. For example:

Teamwork	
Leadership and Management Behaviors	
Leadership	**Management**
Flexing your style to meet the needs of your team's development level	Use the guidelines for the stages of team development.
Recruit, train, and develop team members who have diverse backgrounds to strengthen the team and store results.	Remove obstacles as your team develops through the different stages.
Educate and communicate the value of teamwork.	Follow up on team goals and results.

21th CENTURY LEADERSHIP

Late 20th Century Definition of Leadership: I get others to do what is needed by my authority. I have impact and make things happen.	**21st Century Definition of Leadership:** I create the conditions that motivate everyone to achieve Organizational goals. Things happen through others.
Mindsets:	
I Know	**They Know**
I tell them what to do and think.	I set goals and teach them how to think.
It's up to them (their future is their failure).	It's up to us (their failure is my failure).
I manage their actions.	I create the conditions for them to be successful.
I build relationships so people will do what I want.	I am authentic and genuine in my relationships.
If they aren't getting my message, they aren't listening.	If they aren't getting my message, I'm not communicating effectively.
Results In:	
Short-term efficiency gains	Long-term organizational improvements
Dis-empowerment	Empowerment
Obedience	Self-motivation
Resignation	Inspiration
Fear	Pride

The Trium Group

This is the difference between the 20th century leadership mindset and the 21st century mindset. (I was raised on the 20th century mindset.)

EXERCISE: BREADTH BUILDER

1. Make a list of five areas of the business you "don't know much about."

   a. ____

   b. ____

   c. ____

   d. ____

   e. ____

2. For each, schedule one hour this month to learn: shadow a colleague, read an article, listen to a podcast, or sit with your numbers team.
3. At the end of the month, write down one insight from each area that changes how you think about leadership.
4. Share one of those insights with your team.

CHAPTER 5 VERY IMPORTANT POINTS

- Leaders must understand every lane enough to connect the dots.
- Curiosity drives innovation; comfort breeds blind spots.

- Field time reveals truths reports never will.
- Patterns and micro-observations fuel big breakthroughs.
- Knowledge across functions accelerates smarter, faster decisions.

Chapter 6

TOOL: THE TEAM DIAGNOSTIC

Ask yourself: *Do I lead a dynasty-caliber team, or just a "pretty good" one?*

Measure your team across five factors:

1. **Clarity** — Does every person know the mission, the metrics, and their role?
2. **Capability** — Do they have the skills and training to deliver?
3. **Character** — Do they demonstrate grit, humility, and loyalty?
4. **Chemistry** — Do they trust each other and pull in the same direction?
5. **Consistency** — Do they perform month after month, not just occasionally?

A dynasty-level team scores high in all five. Anything less needs immediate attention.

EXERCISE: TEAM REPORT CARD

Grade your current team A–F across the five Team Diagnostic categories:

- Any **C or below** is a risk to your results.
- Choose **one action this week** to raise each weak grade.
- Share the report card with your leadership team and **own the fixes together**.

CHAPTER 6 VERY IMPORTANT POINTS

- Teams determine your ceiling; leaders who build dynasties never settle for capable.
- Strategy, structure, and talent create predictable performance.
- Relentless alignment prevents drift.
- Ruthless prioritization keeps teams focused on what actually moves the needle.
- The strongest leaders export talent. They don't hoard it.

Chapter 7

CHAPTER 7 VERY IMPORTANT POINTS

- Systems, coaching, and standards elevate average people into consistent performers.

- Clear expectations, real scoreboards, and accountability produce predictable wins.
- The Coaching Loop is non-negotiable for skill development.
- Flow state matters. Focus, resilience, presence, confidence, and gratitude drive performance.
- Leaders create environments where growth is expected and supported.

Chapter 8

EXERCISE: LIFT THE MIDDLE

1. **Pick three "average" performers** on your team.
2. **Identify their weakest "E"** from Jack Welch's 4 E's: Energy, Energize, Edge, or Execute.
3. **Choose one targeted action** this week (training, coaching, feedback, or recognition) to lift that trait.
4. **Review progress in thirty days** and repeat the cycle.

EXERCISE: BUILD YOUR SCOREBOARD

1. Identify the five numbers that drive your business.
2. Make them visible to your entire team. Post them where everyone can see.
3. Review them weekly with your leadership team.

4. Hold one conversation this week where you use the numbers to coach, not just opinions.

Accountability isn't a punishment. It's the foundation of performance.

CHAPTER 8 VERY IMPORTANT POINTS

- Clarity comes from metrics; what gets measured drives performance.
- Accountability aligns teams and fuels a culture of ownership.
- Great leaders act on data, not excuses; inspection precedes correction.
- Excellence dies where mediocrity is accepted; reject "close enough."
- Your standards shape your culture; model urgency, drive, and intensity.

Chapter 9

TOOL: THE CULTURE CONTRACT

Use these three questions as your daily filter:

1. **What am I tolerating right now that undermines my culture?**

2. **What behavior am I rewarding, intentionally or not?**
3. **What's one standard I can reassert today?**

What you tolerate today becomes your culture tomorrow.

EXERCISE: ZERO TOLERANCE WEEK

For the next fourteen days, pick one behavior you've been tolerating that hurts your culture.

1. Announce to your team that this behavior is no longer acceptable.
2. Enforce it consistently for fourteen days. No exceptions.
3. At the end of the two weeks, evaluate: How did the team respond? Did standards rise? Did respect increase?

Repeat this process with a new behavior each month. Over time, your culture will shift dramatically

CHAPTER 9 VERY IMPORTANT POINTS

- What you tolerate today becomes your culture tomorrow.
- Standards are enforced in the uncomfortable moments, not the easy ones.
- Accountability is clarity, and clarity is kindness.
- Stop protecting feelings if it means compromising excellence.
- The scoreboard never lies, and neither does your performance.

Chapter 10

TOOL: THE INTEGRATION MAP

Instead of asking, *"How do I balance everything?"* ask: *What matters most right now, and how do I show up fully?*

1. **Identify the Season** — Work surge? Family focus? Personal growth?
2. **Clarify Priorities** — Choose your top 3 (not 10).
3. **Set Boundaries** — Define when and where you'll be fully engaged.
4. **Communicate Clearly** — Let your team and family know what to expect.
5. **Review Often** — Adjust as seasons shift.

EXERCISE: BROWN BAG DRILL

1. Before your next shift, meeting, or training session, write down everything on your mind: personal stress, unfinished tasks, worries.
2. Fold the paper, put it in a bag or drawer.
3. Say out loud: *"I'll pick this up later. Right now, my team gets my best."*
4. Walk into the room focused, present, and all-in.

Repeat daily for a week. Notice how much more energy and clarity you bring when you check the bag at the door.

CHAPTER 10 VERY IMPORTANT POINTS

- Balance is a myth; clarity and intentional focus create real harmony.
- Seasons shift, so should your priorities; be all-in where it matters most.
- Harmony means trade-offs, not guilt; success requires conscious sacrifices.
- Presence beats perfection; quality of engagement outweighs quantity.
- Leave the baggage at the door; your team needs your leadership, not your stress.

Chapter 11

TOOL: THE LEVERAGE LADDER

1. **Do It Yourself** — You carry the weight. No leverage.
2. **Delegate Tasks** — You hand off work, but keep ownership.
3. **Develop People** — You build leaders who can own outcomes.
4. **Export Talent** — You send those leaders into bigger roles and new markets.
5. **Multiply Influence** — Your systems, culture, and people expand results without your direct involvement.

Climbing this ladder is the essence of leadership growth.

EXERCISE: LEVERAGE AUDIT

1. Write down your top ten weekly tasks.
2. Circle which ones could be delegated or taught to someone else.
3. Identify one person you could develop to take over a key responsibility.
4. Build a thirty-day plan to train and empower them.

CHAPTER 11 VERY IMPORTANT POINTS

- Success scales only when leaders multiply themselves through others.
- Your influence is measured by how many people can perform without you in the room.
- Developing leaders is not optional; it is the job.
- Holding onto tasks out of fear chokes growth and creates bottlenecks.
- Legacy is built through people, not personal output.

Chapter 12

TOOL: THE RESPONSIBILITY EQUATION

Responsibility = Ownership + Accountability + Service

- **Ownership** — The willingness to say, *This is mine to solve.*

- **Accountability** — The desire to measure results and face reality.
- **Service** — The commitment to put the team and mission above yourself.

Titles expire. **Responsibility endures.**

TOOL: OPERATING SYSTEM FOR MANAGERS

1. Have a plan
2. Communicate effectively
3. Build culture
4. Lead by example
5. Coach constantly
6. Be present

Details matter.

EXERCISE

1. **Schedule It**
    - A fifteen-to-thirty-minute monthly one-on-one with each team member.
    - Make it recurring. Non-negotiable.
2. **Prep for It**
    - Review last month's notes and numbers.
    - Think about their *personal* and professional goals.

3. **Run It Like This**
   - **Start Personal:** "How are you doing?" "What's new outside the club?"
   - **Get Tactical:** "Where are you winning?" "What's blocking you?"
   - **Coach Up:** Feedback, challenge, clarity.
   - **End With Support:** "What do you need from me?"
4. **Track It**
   - Take a note.
   - Follow up next month.

Bonus Tip: If you don't know their spouse/partner's name, their kids' names, their hobbies, or what lights them up, you have homework to do.

EXERCISE: RESPONSIBILITY REFLECTION

1. List three areas where you currently carry responsibility.
2. Ask: *Am I owning these fully, or am I relying on my title to cover me?*
3. Identify one area where you've been avoiding responsibility.
4. Take one action this week to step up and own it, without waiting for recognition.

Leadership isn't about the stripes on your sleeve or the letters after your name. **It's about what you carry when it counts.**

CHAPTER 12 VERY IMPORTANT POINTS

- Titles sit on paper; responsibility lives in action.
- Real leaders lean in before recognition and stay accountable after mistakes.
- Presence, discipline, and example outrank authority every time.
- Respect is earned through consistency, not hierarchy.
- Leadership begins the moment you choose to own the outcome.
- Get to know your team.

Chapter 13

TOOL: THE CHARACTER COMPASS

Check yourself against these four directions:

1. **North: Integrity** — Do you keep promises and honor commitments?
2. **East: Humility** — Do you listen, learn, and give credit?
3. **South: Consistency** — Do you show up the same way, day after day?
4. **West: Courage** — Do you make the hard calls even when they're unpopular?

If your compass points are aligned, your leadership will stay true.

THE CHARACTER COMPASS

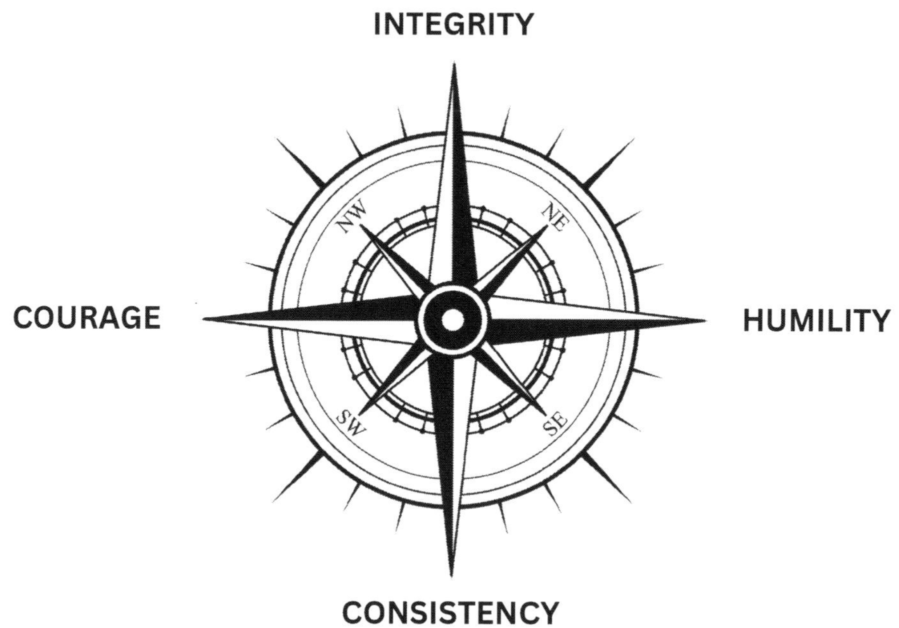

EXERCISE: THE MIRROR TEST

Tonight, look in the mirror and ask yourself:

1. Did I model the behaviors I expect from my team today?
2. Did I give credit where it was due?
3. Did I own my mistakes without excuses?
4. Did I make at least one hard decision instead of avoiding it?

If the answer is "no" to any, write down how you'll correct it tomorrow. Repeat this exercise for 30 days. Character is built through daily discipline.

CHAPTER 13 VERY IMPORTANT POINTS

- Success scales only when leaders multiply themselves through others.
- Your influence is measured by how many people can perform without you in the room.
- Developing leaders is not optional; it is the job.
- Holding onto tasks out of fear chokes growth and creates bottlenecks.
- Legacy is built through people, not personal output.

Chapter 14

TOOL: THE HUMANITY CHECK

Ask yourself these questions weekly:

1. **Am I approachable?** Do people feel safe bringing me problems?
2. **Am I honest?** Do I admit when I don't know or when I'm wrong?
3. **Am I balanced?** Do I allow humor, humility, and grace in my leadership?
4. **Am I connected?** Do I know something about my people beyond their job description?

If you can't say yes to each of these questions, you're leading from a pedestal, not from the trenches.

EXERCISE: THE VULNERABILITY SHARE

At your next team meeting, take five minutes to share one mistake you've made recently, what you learned, and how you corrected it.

1. Keep it short and honest.
2. Invite your team to share their own lessons learned.
3. Celebrate the growth, not just the outcome.

Do this once a month. You'll be amazed how much loyalty and connection grow when people see that it's okay to be human.

EXERCISE: COMMUNICATION IS KEY

Write your "three true things" you will share with your team this quarter.

1. ____
2. ____
3. ____

CHAPTER 14 VERY IMPORTANT POINTS

- Being human and real builds far more trust than pretending to be invincible.
- Admitting mistakes, asking for help, and owning your role in outcomes is not weakness; it is leadership.

- Vulnerability, humor, and grace keep you and your team grounded, connected, and resilient.
- Great leaders adapt their communication and coaching to how each person learns best.
- You are always on stage as a leader, so your behavior must consistently match the standards you expect from others.

CRUNCH

ABOUT THE AUTHOR

A United States Marine who became one of the most influential operators in the fitness industry, Rowley built his career on grit, discipline, humility, and the belief that leadership decides everything. His life reflects a simple truth: No one is coming, and the people who win are the ones willing to step up, take responsibility, and drive results when everyone else is waiting.

Rowley's story begins with service. Eight years in the Marine Corps, including assignments with the Marine Corps Embassy Security Group and a deployment during the Persian Gulf War, shaped the foundation of who he became. The Corps taught him clarity, urgency, accountability, and the mindset to move forward under pressure. Those principles became the backbone of his entire leadership philosophy. But it wasn't until he transitioned back into civilian life that he learned one of his most important lessons: You cannot lead civilians like you lead Marines. You must translate drive into coaching, standards into systems, and purpose into daily tasks that others can follow.

Starting at the bottom as a rookie sales counselor, Rowley learned the fitness business the hard way: dialing from windowless rooms, selling memberships face-to-face, studying every inch of operations, and climbing through every level of responsibility. He didn't rise because of pedigree or credentials. He rose because he outworked, out-prepared, and out-led everyone around him. Those years built the intuition, character, and relentless curiosity that would define his leadership.

When Crunch Fitness hit bankruptcy in 2009, Rowley didn't inherit a well-oiled machine. He inherited a broken one. What followed was one of the strongest turnarounds in the industry. He established new standards, revitalized the culture, closed underperforming clubs, rebuilt systems, and recruited leaders who matched the DNA of high performance. He proved that discipline, clarity, and accountability could resurrect a brand and turn it into a global force. But he didn't do all this on his own; he did it with the team he selected to help him win. Today, Crunch stands at over 500 clubs worldwide, a testament to leadership that refuses excuses.

But Rowley's impact goes far beyond numbers. He is known for developing people. For turning everyday performers into capable, confident leaders. For demanding preparation, ownership, and high standards, while also modeling humility and emotional intelligence. He sees the talent in people before they see it in themselves and pushes them to become the version of themselves capable of carrying the mission forward.

What separates Rowley isn't charisma or position. It's consistency. It's the willingness to make the hard call, to stay hungry when others get comfortable, and to lead from the front. His message is direct: Leadership isn't about waiting to be rescued. Leadership is responsibility. It's action. It's standing up when others shrink back. And it's understanding that culture isn't created by slogans; it's created by behavior, by standards, and by the leader's example.

Jim Rowley's life and leadership are proof that greatness isn't theoretical. It's earned through service, through sacrifice, and through the daily decision to choose the harder path. His journey from Marine to CEO is not a story of luck. It is a story of ownership, resilience, and a relentless commitment to excellence.

CRUNCH

ABOUT CRUNCH FITNESS

Crunch Fitness is more than a gym brand. It is a culture built on determination, inclusivity, and the belief that ordinary people can achieve extraordinary results when leadership, standards, and community come together. From its beginnings in a small New York City studio to becoming one of the fastest growing fitness franchises in the world, Crunch has always stood for one thing: making fitness fun without sacrificing the work it takes to win.

Crunch was born in Greenwich Village, surrounded by creativity, personality, and the raw energy of people who wanted fitness without judgment. That spirit shaped everything. The brand embraced individuality, encouraged self-expression, and welcomed every walk of life. But underneath the irreverence and fun was something even more powerful: a fierce commitment to performance. Crunch proved you can be welcoming without being soft, playful without losing standards, and inclusive without lowering the bar.

When new leadership stepped in during bankruptcy, the mission was not simply to save a gym chain. It was to rebuild a culture. That meant shutting down struggling clubs, resetting expectations, and reintroducing discipline across every level of the business. High standards became the heartbeat of the system. Training got sharper. Systems got cleaner. Accountability became non-negotiable. And the team leaned on a simple truth: Culture beats strategy, but a great culture requires leaders who refuse to tolerate mediocrity.

From those foundational decisions came the modern Crunch: a global network of more than 500 gyms built on humility, consistency, and execution. Franchisees stepped up. Teams elevated. Leaders learned to think like owners, to dig into data, and to own results instead of waiting for rescue. The brand grew, not because of luck, but because people in every market chose to lead with clarity, resilience, and the commitment to finish what they start.

What separates Crunch today is the blend of soul and standards. Members feel the energy the moment they walk in. Franchisees feel the support and the system behind them. Teams feel the pride of being part of a culture that wins. Crunch is playful on the outside, but deeply intentional on the inside. It is a system built to develop leaders, elevate performers, and help everyday people become the strongest version of themselves.

Crunch stands for more than fitness. It stands for ownership, courage, consistency, and the relentless belief that no one is coming: it's up to you. And that belief is what turned a struggling brand into a global force. It is what continues to drive its growth. And it is what makes Crunch one of the most dynamic, disciplined, and exciting fitness organizations in the world.